"*Butterbox Babies* is one of those stories, skillfully researched and written by Halifax CBC Television producer Bette Cahill. It took three years and scores of interviews to unearth one of Atlantic Canada's darkest secrets, but unearth it she did."

— *Saskatoon Star Phoenix*

"*Butterbox Babies* is Bette Cahill's exhaustively researched exposé of the Ideal Maternity Home in East Chester. Cahill, a Halifax journalist, reveals horrifying tales of abuse, illegal adoptions and even murder."

— *Halifax Daily News*

"Cahill has unearthed a complex story that mixes community service with profiteering, moral uplift with evil."

— *Vancouver Sun*

Photo of babies and "staff" from the Ideal Maternity Home, published in the Home's official brochure.

Butterbox Babies

Baby Sales
Baby Deaths

New Revelations 15 Years Later

Bette L. Cahill

Fernwood Publishing
Halifax, Nova Scotia

Design: Brenda Conroy
Printed and bound in Canada by Hignell Printing Limited

Published in Canada by Fernwood Publishing
Site 2A, Box 5, 32 Oceanvista Lane
Black Point, Nova Scotia, B0J 1B0
and 324 Clare Avenue, Winnipeg, Manitoba, R3L 1S3
www.fernwoodpublishing.ca

Fernwood Publishing Company Limited gratefully acknowledges the financial support of the Department of Canadian Heritage, the Nova Scotia Department of Tourism and Culture and the Canada Council for the Arts for our publishing program.

Fernwood Publishing thanks Nova Scotia Archives and Records Management for the use of the photos on pages 17, 87, 89 and 147.

Library and Archives Canada Cataloguing in Publication

Cahill, Bette L.
Butterbox babies : baby sales, baby deaths : new revelations fifteen years later / Bette L. Cahill. -- 2nd ed.

ISBN-13: 978-1-55266-216-8 (bound)
ISBN-13: 978-1-55266-213-7 (pbk.)
ISBN-10: 1-55266-216-0 (bound)
ISBN-10: 1-55266-213-6 (pbk.)

1. Ideal Maternity Home. 2. Maternity homes--Nova Scotia--East Chester. 3. Illegitimate children--Care--Nova Scotia--East Chester. 4. Unmarried mothers--Care--Nova Scotia--East Chester. 5. Adoption--Corrupt practices--Nova Scotia. I. Title.

HV700.5.C34 2006 362.83'92850971623 C2006-903720-5

For my mother

Contents

Acknowledgements

The success of a book such as this depends heavily on the support and encouragement of others. For this I am eternally grateful to my mother Rita MacKenzie and my brother John Cahill. My sister-in-law, Lin Cahill, did a fantastic critique of the manuscript. To Janet Francis of Halifax, my life long friend and confidant, your help is appreciated more than you know. A special thank you to my partner-in-crime, Naomi Matthews, who read and commented on the manuscript and helped in other ways too numerous to mention.

Many thanks to the team at Fernwood publishing: Brenda Conroy, Beverley Rach, Debbie Mathers, Cynthia Martin and Errol Sharpe. Your advice and professionalism is greatly appreciated.

Newsroom colleagues at CBC Halifax also contributed. Jim Nunn first told me about the Ideal Maternity Home; Jamie Lipsit assigned me the first story. Geoff D'Eon and Nancy Waugh both allowed me leave from work to complete the project. The CBC's Regional Director for the Maritimes Ron Crocker gave generously of his time to help edit and develop the original chapters as they took shape. It was his advice, his enthusiasm for the story and his confidence in me that helped make it all possible. While all these people contributed, the responsibility for any errors in this book rests with me.

Preface

The story of baby deaths and black-market adoptions in Nova Scotia surfaced in the fall of 1988, when Malcolm Phillips, a reporter with a local paper on the South Shore, contacted the CBC television newsroom in Halifax. He said he knew of a secret baby burial ground in the area, and that babies buried there had died of neglect at the Ideal Maternity Home more than fifty years earlier. People in the Chester area had told Phillips about the burial ground, but he felt the story was too legally sensitive for him to write about. As a reporter with CBC Television News at the time, I was assigned the story.

My research put me in touch with numerous people who had been connected with the Home. Over a period of months I travelled across Canada and the United States to find women who had stayed there and who had been born there. Some of the people I located — acquaintances of Lila and William, former employees, adoptive parents and birth parents — were reluctant to talk about their experiences. They have been given pseudonyms and appear in this book as Stella Mulgrave, Vivian Brown, Anna MacKenna, Eleanor Marriott, Kate Davidson, Freda MacLaren, Mary Barton and Cyril Covey. The identities of other valuable sources will remain private, as requested.

Stella Mulgrave, an elderly woman living in Chester Basin and a former employee at the Maternity Home, confided in me about "atrocities" she had witnessed there, but was afraid to be interviewed at length. Throughout the course of my research, I spoke with Stella on the phone several times and visited her once, briefly. She was always edgy, always reluctant to talk. Finally, she agreed to an in-depth interview, but before it took place, I received a phone call from the Royal Canadian Mounted Police in Chester asking that I have no further contact with Stella. Someone had threatened to harm her if she spoke to me. As I drove past Stella's house on my next visit to Chester I noticed I was being followed. I decided Stella's safety should come first and abandoned the interview idea. Stella's experiences at the Ideal Maternity Home have never been told.

The toughest interview was with Joy Young, Lila and William's daughter, who lives in a small fishing village outside of Halifax. Tormented all her life by allegations against her parents, she was not surprisingly unwilling to be interviewed. I visited Joy on a cold winter morning in January 1989. For two hours we sat uncomfortably at her kitchen table sipping tea and making conversation. She finally opened up, but so feared publicity that she asked that certain statements remain off the record. I have respected her wishes.

During my research I read countless newspaper clippings, court documents, letters and other valuable material. Unfortunately, the Youngs' personal papers and adoption records were lost in a fire in 1962, so details about the Home's operations, particularly in the early years, have been lost. My research was made easier, however, by the discovery of papers in the walls of the East Chester Inn, Lila and William Young's former residence. In 1989, in the midst of renovations, workmen found an assortment of bills and letters written to the Youngs years ago by girls who stayed at the Ideal Maternity Home. Some letters, on thin, yellowed paper, were barely legible; others provided valuable information. Many of the letters and documents contain spelling and grammatical errors; they appear unchanged in this book.

The Public Archives of Nova Scotia offered a wide range of documents, including the Young's advertising brochures from the 1930s and 1940s. These pamphlets yielded crucial insights as well as photographs of the Youngs, their supporters and the

Maternity Home. In the absence of certain trial records, I relied on newspaper stories and archival documents to help re-create the court cases. For the 1947 libel trial, for example, I took advantage of almost verbatim testimony in the daily newspapers.

But in the end it was the cooperation and assistance of the people throughout Canada and the United States who survived the Ideal Maternity Home that made the telling of this story possible. To those men and women I wish to convey my most sincere appreciation.

— Bette L. Cahill
Halifax, Nova Scotia

Prologue

A young woman in Nova Scotia gives birth to a child out of wedlock. A childless couple in New Jersey desperately searches for a baby to adopt. These people never meet. But their lives become forever linked through a tiny baby girl. Natalie, that baby, spent the first two years of her life at the Ideal Maternity Home on Canada's rocky east coast. She was adopted in August 1945 by Louis and Mabel Goldman of Newark. Her father was a lawyer, her mother a teacher, both loving parents who called Natalie their chosen child.

Natalie was only six and living with her parents in Maplewood, New Jersey, when she threatened to run away and find her birth mother. It was then that her mother informed her that her biological mother had died when she was an infant and her father, a pilot, was killed in a plane crash during the war.

In the years that followed, Natalie learned to keep silent about how she imagined the Queen of England to be her mother, how she had nightmares in which her "real" mother would snatch her away from the only parents she had ever known, how she longed for a photograph that would let her see herself in another's face. Natalie grew up hiding feelings of abandonment and guilt, loss and sorrow.

As a mother of two in her early fifties and living in New Jersey, Natalie finally decided to confront her past. She hired a private investigator, who, in a short time, delivered the devastating news that Natalie's birth mother was dead. Violet Hamilton had been living in New Brunswick and had died just eleven years earlier, in 1986. "The pain of that loss was overwhelming.

There had been a window of opportunity when I could have known her, if only I had searched earlier."

Joy began to overshadow pain when Natalie learned that after fifty-three years she no longer had to consider herself an only child. Four of Violet's children, three brothers and a sister, still lived in Canada.

Natalie felt as though she had won the Olympic gold four times over, one medal for each sibling. Natalie, it turned out, was the baby of the family. Before long, telephone lines were buzzing, photos were exchanged and meetings arranged. Natalie says the real treasure for her was finding her older sister Shirley, who, when she learned about Natalie, got in her car and drove directly to New Jersey, where the two spent the July 4th holiday together. "She became my sister, my mother, my best friend, my confidant. I cherish her to this day."

The sisters kept in touch and met again the following month, at the 1997 reunion of survivors of the Ideal Maternity Home in Nova Scotia. "In Canada, I found myself," she says, a

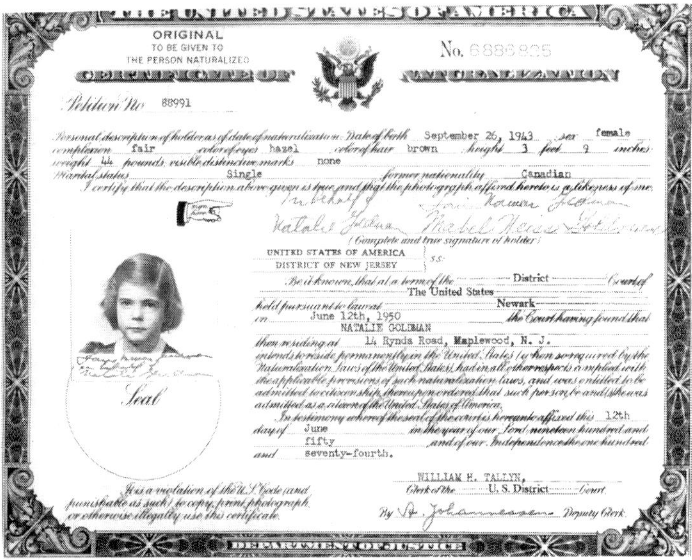

ORIGINAL
TO BE GIVEN TO
THE PERSON NATURALIZED

Petition No. 88991

Personal description of holder as of date of naturalization: Date of birth September 26, 1943 sex female
complexion fair color of eyes hazel color of hair brown height 3 feet 9 inches
weight 44 pounds; visible distinctive marks none
Marital status Single former nationality Canadian
I certify that the description above given is true, and that the photograph affixed hereto is a likeness of me.

(Complete and true signature of holder)

UNITED STATES OF AMERICA
DISTRICT OF NEW JERSEY } ss:

Be it known, that at a term of the District Court of The United States held pursuant to law at Newark on June 12th, 1950 the Court having found that NATALIE GOLDMAN then residing at 14 Rynda Road, Maplewood, N. J. intends to reside permanently in the United States (when so required by the Naturalization Laws of the United States), had in all other respects complied with the applicable provisions of such naturalization laws, and was entitled to be admitted to citizenship, thereupon ordered that such person be and (s)he was admitted as a citizen of the United States of America.

In testimony whereof the seal of the court is hereunto affixed this 12th day of June in the year of our Lord nineteen hundred and fifty and of our Independence the one hundred and seventy-fourth.

Seal

WILLIAM H. TALLYN,
Clerk of the U. S. District Court.
By Deputy Clerk.

It is a violation of the U.S. Code (and punishable as such) to copy, print, photograph, or otherwise illegally use this certificate.

DEPARTMENT OF JUSTICE

Document confirming Natalie Hamilton's U.S. citizenship, issued in 1950, when she was seven.

Natalie Hamilton's reunion with her family in Nova Scotia in August 1997. Left to right: David, Shirley, Jim, Natalie and Kenny.

little teary-eyed, "and I think that's where I was. I was always there." While in Chester, Natalie visited the Casa Blanca Guest Home and discovered Mabel Goldman's name in an old registry. The elderly owner of the guest home, Isabel Marshall, told Natalie how adoptive parents walked between rows of cribs — girls on one side, boys on the other — and picked out their babies as if they were picking out apples at the supermarket.

Natalie paid tribute to her past by laying a wreath of violets and roses at a monument to all of the Ideal Maternity Home babies, living and dead. The violets represented her birth mother's name, the roses her adoptive mother's favourite flower. After the memorial dedication, Natalie watched her sister Shirley wander off alone toward the adjacent property, where the Ideal Maternity Home once stood. "I was crying for myself because of all I had gone through," Natalie recalls. "I had tears of sadness and joy. My sister was crying silently, not for herself, but for our mother and all she had gone through as a young woman forced to give up her baby and dying so many years later, never knowing what happened to her."

Natalie's three brothers also attended the reunion in Chester that summer. They comforted her as she shed fifty-three years worth of tears. She had finally come home to confront her new reality. "Well little girl," her eldest brother said, "it took you a very long time, but you finally found your way home."

PART I

Birth of a Business 1928–1939

Make your's

A Happy Home By Adopting A Baby - - -

When I first saw you I was afraid to meet you.
When I first met you I was afraid to like you.
When I first liked you I was afraid to love you.
Now that I love you I am afraid to lose you.

Natalie Hamilton
Ideal Maternity Home survivor

Chapter 1

William and Lila

On the two-lane highway winding along Nova Scotia's South Shore a sign signals the turn-off to Fox Point, a tiny fishing village that in 1887 was home to Bessie Coolen, a gentle woman believed to be the area's first Seventh-day Adventist. When Bessie was just a teenager living in nearby Seabright she belonged to a group of Seventh-day Adventists based in Tantallon, the second-oldest Seventh-day Adventist congregation in Canada. Salem Coolen, a Fox Point fisherman, used to row back and forth across St. Margaret's Bay to court Bessie. Eventually they married and settled in a large white-and-green farmhouse in Fox Point. Salem promised to convert to the Adventist faith after the marriage, but it soon became apparent

Lila and William Young, owners of the Ideal Maternity Home.

he was having difficulty respecting the Sabbath. Struck with paralysis, he vowed that if the Lord healed him, he would rest on the "seventh day." Salem was cured, so the story goes, and he kept his promise.

Salem and Bessie raised eight sons and three daughters. There was no Seventh-day Adventist church in Fox Point, so Bessie conducted services in her parlour, reading the Bible to her family and friends. Her lessons were clear and simple: salvation was the goal; clean living the way. Marginalized by some mainstream Christians because of their strict, literal interpretation of the Bible, Seventh-day Adventists proudly conform to unwavering beliefs and behaviour. Caffeine, smoking, drinking and going to dances or movies were frowned on, as were clothes and jewellery that "aroused the lust of the flesh." The Seventh-day Adventist diet, adopted by the Coolens, was also strict. Vegetarian foods, those that "God ordained in the Garden of Eden," were preferred.

Bessie's family was prominent in this small seaside village, which was also home to the Shatfords, Westhavers and Harnish's. Entering Fox Point from the north, the bright blue waters of St. Margaret's Bay are on the left; on the right, mailboxes mark long driveways climbing to sturdy wooden houses. Some of the families lived in houses built by their fathers or grandfathers more than a century earlier and have lived alongside one another for generations.

Like many men in the village, the Coolens fished for tuna, mackerel and lobster that they sold to the local lobster pound or the big buyers in Halifax, thirty miles away. All of the Coolen children were taught at the two-room school in the village, where the value of a good education was instilled in every pupil at an early age, but it was their religion that guided them throughout their lives. The Coolens, like other Seventh-day Adventists in the area, were fundamentalists who awaited the second coming of Christ. They held Saturday, not Sunday, as their day of rest. About half of the Coolen children remained committed Seventh-day Adventists throughout their lives.

When the Coolens were not studying the Bible or attending school, they loaded up their boats and went fishing for giant bluefin tuna, which they packed on ice and delivered to steamers travelling to Boston and New York; they salted mackerel for Halifax merchants exporting to the West Indies. Family members also held respected positions in the community. Two of the boys, Frederick and Roland, became justices of the peace, Robie was a boat builder and the village blacksmith, and Freeman was a doctor. Freeman spent much of his professional life in the U.S., in Oklahoma and Illinois; later in life he returned to Fox Point, practising medicine part-time from his home.

The eldest girl, Lila Gladys Coolen, dreamed of being a respected teacher in the village, who could shape and mold the minds of impressionable youngsters. Soon after finishing school she began teaching in Fox Point, where some of her former students recall her as generous and compassionate, but according to her youngest brother, Cecil, Lila could also be headstrong, even as a child.

Travelling preachers also made an impression on the Coolen family. Lila was twenty-six when she met and was immediately impressed by William Peach Young, an unordained Seventh-day Adventist minister from Memramcook, New Brunswick. William was a self-designated medical missionary, caring for the sick while spreading the gospel along the South Shore. In 1925, William stopped at one the area's few meeting places for Seventh-day Adventists, the Coolen home in Fox Point, and it was here that he first laid eyes on Lila Coolen. The night he was supposed to leave Nova Scotia, there was a thunderstorm and his train was delayed. He stayed another day and began courting Lila.

William was born in LaGrande, Oregon, on January 11, 1898, the son of a well-known Seventh-day Adventist clergyman. The family moved to various cities and towns in the U.S. and Canada, following their father from posting to posting. William attended public school in Austin, Manitoba, and the Maritime Academy in Memramcook. With the aim of becoming a medical missionary overseas, he enrolled at the Oshawa Missionary College in Ontario and later at the Medical Evangelists College in California.

William still hoped to go abroad when he met and fell in love with Lila Coolen in 1925. But Lila soon became pregnant and the nine months that followed were difficult and painful because of a serious back ailment. She recovered after the birth, as did the sickly baby, a boy named William. William, Sr., who by now had abandoned his dream of travelling abroad, discovered a new interest after seeing a chiropractor successfully treat Lila.

The Youngs moved their small family to Chicago, where William enrolled at the National College of Chiropractic and, in December 1927, he graduated. That same year Lila graduated from the National School of Obstetrics and Midwifery. They returned to Nova Scotia and in February 1928 opened "The Life and Health Sanitarium — Where the Sick Get Well." They worked out of their four-bedroom cottage in East Chester, a fishing and lumbering village forty miles southwest of Halifax and twelve miles from Fox Point. This rural site was chosen in part because a local businessman had agreed to lend them $2,700 to purchase the property. The Youngs barely had enough money of their own to buy cots for the patients to sleep on.

At this point in their lives William and Lila fit admirably into the Seventh-day Adventist tradition of looking after the physical, spiritual and social needs of others. Lila started delivering babies and within a year the Youngs were specializing in maternity services, largely for unwed mothers. Their business became known as the Ideal Maternity Home and Sanitarium. William was the superintendent, Lila the director.

Eleanor Marriott, who lived on a farm near the Maternity Home, first met Lila and William when they appeared at her door one night. "Lila was carrying a small child in her arms, and she held out an empty pitcher and asked to borrow milk," Eleanor recalls. "It seemed like they came from nowhere, and the next thing I knew, they were running a maternity home."

Chapter 2

Mothers' Refuge

In the early 1930s, more than a few of the girls who found their way to Nova Scotia's Ideal Maternity Home came from wealthy, influential families. Typically, a girl from a well-to-do family was said to be leaving home to attend finishing school, when her destination was, in fact, the Ideal Maternity Home. The average age of the girls was 17. In the beginning, the Home was quiet and inconspicuous, with only a few girls staying there at any one time. Gradually, it grew in popularity. Off and on in the early 1930s, the following advertisement appeared in the Halifax *Chronicle*, circulated across the province:

IDEAL MATERNITY HOME
"Mothers' Refuge" also department for girls.
NO PUBLICITY.
INFANTS home in connection.
Write for literature. East Chester, N.S.

The Home the Youngs started with in East Chester in 1928.

The literature included brochures promising to shield "Expectant Mothers from gossip while recognizing that one cannot lift another up by calling them down." The last statement would have been particularly appealing as it showed a compassion and tolerance far ahead of its time. Many others who ended up at the Ideal Maternity Home were poor, uneducated and vulnerable. Whether rich or poor the punishment was the same for all. If a girl became pregnant out of wedlock, she would be shunned by her family and friends. Illegitimacy not only brought public shame but also caused economic degradation, often forcing the disposal of the unwelcome child.

Contraception was not the answer either. It was illegal under the Criminal Code in the 1930s. Men could surreptitiously obtain sheaths or condoms, but their relatively high price, doctors' warnings that they could cause irritation and their association with prostitution discouraged their use.

Furthermore, birth control was generally seen as a woman's responsibility. As a result, women not wanting to become pregnant had to rely on abstinence or withdrawal. When the latter failed, they had few choices. Some resorted to pills and potions they read about in newspaper advertisements, which fraudulently claimed the products would bring about abortions. The most desperate tried to induce miscarriages or arranged clandestine abortions, which were inevitably dangerous and frequently fatal.

Abortion was generally unavailable to poor and working-class women; few could afford those doctors willing to break the law for a price. As a result, amateur, self-induced abortions were common. The least harmful ones involved hot baths, violent exercise or consumption of large quantities of gin. If the pregnancy continued, women resorted to more perilous methods, such as homemade douches of Lysol, turpentine or carbide. In their most frantic state, they inserted a variety of objects such as catheters, lead pencils, knitting needles, crochet hooks or slippery elm through the cervix, causing bleeding, even haemorrhaging.

It was only after such attempts failed that poor women turned to abortionists. In the mid-1930s, a Halifax obstetrician, Dr. Edward K. MacLellan, reported that about one-third of all maternal deaths resulted from peritonitis, an infection of the abdominal lining sometimes caused by unsterilized medical instruments used during abortions. A colleague, Dr. W.D. Forrest, termed such abortions "all too prevalent" in Nova Scotia.

A specialist in obstetrics and gynecology at Halifax's Victoria General Hospital in the early 1920s through to the 1940s, Harold Benge Atlee, was furious that otherwise healthy young women died because of illegal abortions carried out under unsanitary conditions. In the pre-antibiotic days, Dr. Atlee saw many women so ill from sepsis that they failed to respond to blood transfusions or antibacterial sulfa drugs. Seeing the tragic results of criminal abortions, Dr. Atlee argued for women's right to legal abortions conducted by skilled physicians, under sterile conditions.

Pregnant women who died during unsuccessful abortions often cast unintentional humiliation upon their families when their death notice appeared in the newspapers. Thus we know that Jessie Gould, a waitress at the Cadillac Hotel in Toronto, died of acute septic peritonitis in 1908; Mary Ellen Janes of Victoria died of blood poisoning in 1895; Kate Hutchinson Gardener, a chambermaid at the Tecumseh Hotel in London, Ontario, died of an overdose of chloroform in 1878. Women from wealthier families could rely on the discretion of private maternity homes. Some performed abortions; others arranged adoptions or care for the infants.

Although most of the homes operated quietly, some were known to the police. In Saskatchewan, for example, the authorities knew of two homes for unmarried mothers: one in Regina and another near Prince Edward. During the Second World War, the owner of the Regina home, a middle-aged woman, was convicted of performing an illegal abortion and sent to prison for a year.

There was another alternative for unwed pregnant women.

They could enter a charitable government-supported home to deliver their babies. These homes requested the mothers pay a small monthly fee for room and board, although an inability to pay would not prevent admission. The homes, operated by charities, were aligned with the Catholic or Protestant churches and were moralistic and austere. Moreover, the institutions — of which there was only a handful in Nova Scotia — could scarcely handle what was obviously a growing problem. For those women who decided to bear and keep their babies, there was little community sympathy. It would be another twenty years before the Nova Scotia government recognized the need for social-welfare programs for unmarried mothers.

Given these circumstances, the Ideal Maternity Home seemed like a blessing. Girls could go there in secrecy, have their babies and place them for adoption — no questions asked. To get to this haven, they could take the MacKenzie Line bus from Halifax that stopped in front of the Home every morning and night. Or they could take the Canadian National Railways train that passed through East Chester six days a week. Lila Young always greeted the girls personally. A portly woman with swarthy skin and dark hair often pulled back into a bun, Lila was cheerful and accommodating. She was also business-like. Many of the girls soon grew afraid of her. "She was a large woman," recalls Violet Hatt Eisenhauer, who once stayed there. "She had an overwhelming presence and a great sense of power. She could strike terror into people. No one dared challenge her."

William, solidly built, with steel-rimmed glasses and a pencil-thin moustache, was friendly enough, though there were times when he became taciturn and remote. William was able to use his chiropractic skills to relieve backaches resulting from pregnancies. Their religion, everyone agreed, was never far from their hearts. While Lila delivered the babies, William knelt beside the patients and prayed. "William was a wimpy milk-sop type of fellow," recalled Charles Longley, the Youngs' lawyer in the 1940s. "Lila was the boss. She was the one in charge." Former handyman Glen Shatford recalled William as gentle and quiet. "She did all the talking. He just agreed with her. I liked him, though; he was a good fellow to work for. No one ever complained. And she wasn't a bad ol' thing either."

William and Lila charged a hefty price for the privacy they offered and they demanded payment on arrival, between $100 and $200 for room and board, and delivery and adoption of the baby. This was a great deal of money during the Depression, when jobs were scarce and women were pressured to stay out of the work force. Those who could find work outside the home earned half the wages of their male counterparts. Saleswomen at department stores, for example, had to work days and evenings to earn $8 a week. Domestics earned about half that amount. A room in a boarding house in the city rented for $8 a month.

Still, there were always girls in need of the Youngs' services. Upon entering the Home, they usually had to pay an additional $12 for a layette consisting of three dozen diapers, three barracoats, four dresses, four shirts, three wrapping blankets, three pairs of stockings, two pairs of booties, one bonnet and two cards of safety pins. Not surprisingly, many could not afford to pay their bills and had to work off their debt, often for more than a year. This saved William and Lila the expense of hiring housekeeping and child-care staff.

The Home was not exclusively for unmarried women. Indeed, part of its appeal and good reputation depended on the many married women who chose to give birth there, rather than at home or in a hospital in Halifax. Married pregnant women were charged $75 for their delivery and two weeks convalescence. A baby-sitting service cost $2 a week. In the early days this fee was also charged to unwed mothers until their babies were adopted.

The Youngs' entrepreneurial methods also extended into the adoption side of the operation. They provided an advertising brochure to interested couples. With contemporary epigraphs such as "The child of to-day is to become the man or woman of to-morrow" and "Give him a chance," the pamphlet implored couples to "Make your's A Happy Home By Adopting A Baby." The brochure assured prospective adopting parents that the Maternity Home carefully assessed the background of natural parents, emphasizing that this element of the service was free. Further assurances were couched in the hyperbole of the times:

> Special effort is made to place young expectant mothers in the most pleasant surroundings to develop in the child about to be born a happy, lovable disposition, making the child EASY TO ADOPT and a SUNBEAM in the Home

By the mid-1930s the government-supported charitable homes for unwed mothers were pressuring women to take responsibility for their illegitimate babies. They wanted them to stay with their babies in the homes for a minimum six months or take them home when they left. The bonding period did not exist because of compassion: the government's interest was money. Clearly, if the families of unwed mothers took in illegitimate children, the cost would be far less than having the children wards of the court. But some women, unable to keep their children, deserted them at the charitable homes, poor farms or orphanages. Attempts were made to place the children, who became wards of the court, in foster homes, where they were often abused and neglected.

The prevailing wisdom of the day held that it was unwise to allow infants to be adopted at a young age when no one could detect emotional or physical defects. Indeed, during its first eighteen years, the Children's Aid Society of Nova Scotia allowed only twelve adoptions. If adoptions were arranged, the mothers were asked to sign waivers, releasing the infants into the care of the Society; otherwise they kept all rights to their babies.

At the Ideal Maternity Home, the rules were vastly different. Pregnant girls could not enter the Home unless they signed elaborate contracts drafted by William giving him power of attorney and legal authority over their babies and their adoptions. Ultimately, the girls signed away all rights to their infants. If they did not comply within fourteen days of the birth, they had to pay an additional $30. By the time the girls left the Home, their bills often exceeded $300.

Ada Kippen bore a daughter at the Home in 1935 and signed papers guaranteeing that she would "never call for or interfere in any way with the control or affection of the child and forever withdraws all right and title to the child." After the Youngs found a home for her child, Ada had to sign another document.

> In consideration of the love, affection, care and financial support given my child by Mr. And Mrs. Henn, of Halifax, as well as financial circumstances making it necessary for me to part from my child, I hereby relinquish and forever withdraw all claim as her mother and entrust her forever to the care, protection, and support of the said Mr. And Mrs. W.P. Henn who will henceforth act in my stead in the full capacity as parents.

Ada also had to settle the $30 legal bill for the adoption. She was allowed to pay in installments — $8 a month for three months and the balance of $6 in the forth month. If a baby died at the Home, the mother was charged another $20 for the burial. Five dollars went towards a shroud — usually a white flannelette dress — and the remaining $15 went to Lila and William, one of whom was present during burials. The burial fee included a white-pine coffin. "They were lovely butter-boxes, mitered and very, very smooth," Lila once said. "They were always lined with satin. They might have come from a grocer's, but they were always well lined."

By 1933, the Ideal Maternity Home was well established in the East Chester community, and the Youngs were enjoying their success. Often they showed surprising generosity. When they went into the city, Lila would always return with gifts for the children of business associates, perhaps a self-serving gesture, but nonetheless one welcomed by the recipients. There were times when Lila displayed genuine compassion for people in the community. Once she heard about a sick, elderly man who was alone in his home much of the time. Lila barely knew the man but decided to visit him anyway. A relative, who had dropped by on the night she was there, recalls that Lila bathed the man and stayed up with him till dawn, when he died.

Clearly, Lila had the means to make life better for others but not always the motivation — something that worried the Seventh-day Adventists. In 1933, the Youngs had plans to expand the Maternity Home. They wanted the Seventh-day Adventist Church to officially sanction their business. Lila and William had hoped to model their home after the Battle Creek Sanitarium in Michigan, a pioneer Adventist medical institution founded in 1866. The Battle Creek Sanitarium had been the first to publicize Adventists' concepts of health and healing, using hydrotherapy to treat disease. But the church did not see the Ideal Maternity Home as a charitable institution; rather it considered Lila and William entrepreneurs. Therefore, the Youngs' request for church affiliation was rejected.

Chapter 3

Seeds of Conflict

For the first five years, as the Ideal Maternity Home grew in popularity, it benefited from the isolation of its rural setting in East Chester. William and Lila succeeded in keeping their business dealings relatively quiet. The well-to-do people in neighbouring Chester, a tourist enclave for wealthy Americans proud of their large seaside estates and expensive yachts, paid little notice. A home for society's outcasts was the last thing on their minds.

By 1933, however, some people were beginning to take notice. The provincial Liberal Party swept into office that year, and Premier Angus L. MacDonald appointed a surgeon from Bridgewater, Dr. Frank Roy Davis, to the Public Health portfolio. Davis, the son of a Methodist minister, had started practising medicine in 1911 in Petite Rivière, N.S., and later in his hometown of Bridgewater.

Davis was married with two sons and in the beginning did not see himself as a career politician. Before his election, he had enjoyed a large medical practice and was attached to the quiet small-town atmosphere where he could go curling or enjoy a game of golf. It was his supporters in Bridgewater who persuaded a reluctant Davis that he should run for provincial office; once elected and introduced to problems at the Ideal Maternity Home, Frank Davis's peaceful existence soon began to disappear.

Davis was a progressive thinker who believed that social workers should have specialized training, at a time when they were defined as anyone who did charity work in the community. And he believed that children should benefit from every modern medical treatment available — that doctors, not midwives, should deliver babies. During his fifteen years as Public Health minister, Davis oversaw the planning and construction of the new Victoria General Hospital in Halifax and introduced old-age pensions for the blind and free medical treatment for tuberculosis. He also helped open and expand Children's Aid Society offices across Nova Scotia. During the 1936 Moose River, N.S., mine disaster, he became a hero after risking his life to take medical aid to two men trapped in the crumbling gold mine. Davis's fame spread nationwide, as the first coast-to-coast radio broadcast in Canada included ongoing reports from the disaster scene.

As a politician, Davis had a reputation for being stubborn and narrow-minded but dedicated and hard working. A Halifax journalist once said that he left a first impression of a pleasant, easygoing man: "In conversation he likes to deliberate. When he sits down or stands up — when he puts on his glasses, and when he takes a pen in hand — he executes every movement deliberately." Davis might have been forward thinking, but his slow, deliberate execution would eventually characterize his dealings with Lila Young and the Ideal Maternity Home.

From his first day in office, Davis took a particular interest in the Home, for East Chester was in Lunenburg County, the riding he represented. When he heard local gossip that the bodies of babies who died at the Home were sometimes left unattended in a field next to the Seventh-day Adventist cemetery in Fox Point, Davis decided to investigate.

When he approached Lila Young she dismissed the rumours. "On one occasion," she acknowledged, "my husband and I left a body uncovered while we went to look for a workman who was late. We left a boy in charge for a few moments and... well, of necessity he had to be excused." Davis also heard reports that the mortality rate at the Maternity Home was much higher that the five percent average in hospitals across Canada, but without accurate birth and death statistics he had no way to assess it. The reporting of births and deaths had been required by law since 1908; but in rural areas, they often went unreported. Lila knew that such record keeping would have had particular consequences at the Home; filling out the certificates would have meant revealing the surname of the birth mother, undermining the Home's most sought after service: "No publicity."

These unofficial reports of a high death rate were originating from physicians in the Chester area, who had no official business at the Home. They complained that Lila and William were posing as doctors, an allegation supported by William's biography in the *Maritime Reference Book,* a regional *Who's Who* published in 1931. The brief profile, below a photograph of William in graduation cap and gown, called him "Dr. Young" and referred to Lila as an obstetrician. On company letterhead Lila designated herself as "Dr. Lila Young."

"They were both doctors," their daughter Joy would later argue, "and they knew the value of education. We were hardly out of our bed five minutes, and we would be in the classroom. No excuses."

As a chiropractor, William could legally call himself a doctor, but the local physicians believed that he was deliberately misleading girls at the Maternity Home to believe that he was a medical doctor. Before long, though, they focused their attention on Lila. With the medical knowledge she gained by spending long hours studying her brother's medical books, Lila, the midwife, represented a greater threat to the medical establishment than did William, with his beliefs in natural healing.

The practice of midwifery in Nova Scotia and throughout Canada — once the only method of assisted births in many rural locations — began to decline after 1850, when doctors, almost always male, became involved in home deliveries. In the Maritimes, midwives worked for a time in cooperation with home-birth doctors, until the province's road system improved sufficiently that births moved into hospitals. The introduction of blood-transfusion techniques and antibiotics helped make hospital births safer in the 1930s. Hospitals, which in earlier decades had been filthy, crowded, unventilated and prone to epidemics, became cleaner, with increased attention given to proper nutrition and prenatal care.

During the Depression, however, doctors began to lose ground to competent midwives providing less expensive services. These doctors, no doubt frustrated over a loss of considerable income, dismissed midwives as under-educated women playing back-room doctors. Lila Young would have particularly irked the doctors from the Chester area in at least two ways. Lila let it be known that she had a diploma from an American college and publicly claimed that her record of successful deliveries was better than any doctor's. Second, though Halifax midwives had to be certified by the provincial medical board, country midwifery — and Lila — remained unregulated.

The Nova Scotia medical community claimed to accept midwives working alongside doctors during deliveries, but it vehemently opposed midwives handling births — particularly difficult ones — on their own. When the delivery of babies became complicated, Lila Young would have had three choices. She could allow the delivery to take its natural course and accept the outcome, however unfortunate; she could call a doctor; or she could attempt a remedy. Doctors suspected she was doing what they would have done — use high forceps during complicated deliveries — but Lila was not properly qualified. These surgical instruments, long enough to grasp the head of a fetus not yet in the birth canal, were commonly used but required special skill. Indeed, by the end of the 1940s they would no longer be in use in most hospitals because of the danger to both the mother and the fetus.

Lila resented any restrictions on her freedom to practice medicine. John Rafuse, a one-time handyman at the Maternity Home, recalls that she frequently complained about midwives not being able to administer drugs. Only doctors were legally permitted to treat infections with antibiotics, which became readily available in Nova Scotia in the 1940s. However, Lila Young had a reputation as a capable midwife. John Rafuse, who admired Lila's skills, lived with his wife and children in a bungalow near the Maternity Home, and Lila twice delivered their babies. The first delivery went smoothly, but the second did not. John's wife began to haemorrhage, and Lila wanted to take her from the house to the Maternity Home for treatment. He refused, and in a few days his wife recovered. The baby also survived, but the Rafuses called in a doctor to deliver their subsequent children.

In 1933, perhaps in response to mounting pressure, William and Lila engaged a registered nurse, Vallence Dexter Murphy, to work at the Home, but they still would not call in doctors when mothers or babies became ill. This made Frank Davis and his colleagues increasingly suspicious. Most charitable institutions had attending physicians, readily submitted annual reports and asked for only small fees from mothers. The Ideal Maternity Home operated boldly against the grain. If the Youngs would not consult doctors, Davis could assume that women suffering from pelvic infection were not receiving antibiotics, childhood illnesses such as rickets, colds and conjunctivitis were not being properly treated, and babies were not being immunized against such life-threatening diseases as whooping cough, diphtheria, scarlet fever and smallpox.

He concluded that the only way to monitor the Youngs' operation was through inspections, like those already conducted periodically at the church-run charitable maternity homes supported by government. But the inspections revealed little, so Davis changed his tack. He ordered the deputy registrar of births and deaths in Chester to deny the Youngs burial certificates until the RCMP had investigated each death. This strategy was not foolproof, as the Youngs were believed to be burying babies without proper documents. Eventually Lila and William requested a certificate, and Davis got his chance for a closer examination of the Home.

Without effective provincial laws controlling practices and accommodation at private maternity homes, Davis could bring charges only if an RCMP investigation uncovered some criminal wrongdoing. The first investigation failed to reveal foul play.

It focused on a stillbirth at the Home on August 16, 1934. Lila's request for a burial certificate was denied, but instead of carrying out a fast, efficient investigation, authorities let the baby's body remain at the Maternity Home, unburied, for three weeks. It was Lila who eventually informed Davis that the body was still there and was jeopardizing the health of the residents. This mismanagement by the police would come back to haunt Frank Davis.

No other deaths at the Home came to Davis's attention between late 1934 and early 1936, although the Home was becoming increasingly popular — and illegitimacy an ever-larger problem. About seventy babies had been born at the Home in the first five years; in 1935 and 1936, another eighty babies were born there. Given an average of about $150 in fees per mother, William and Lila were grossing about $6,000 annually, when the average income for other rural Nova Scotia families during the Depression was measured in the hundreds.

With girls from Halifax to Montreal arriving regularly, and with their own family growing, the Youngs enlarged their Maternity Home bit by bit. William did many of the renovations himself. According to his daughter, Joy, he was a skilled cabinet-maker. And he usually had help from the handymen who worked at the Home on and off during the 1930s: Aubrey Murphy (nurse Vallence's husband), John Rafuse, Glen Shatford and George Westhaver.

George Westhaver would visit the Home on Saturday nights, after the Sabbath, to meet girls, and he eventually married one who had been staying there. John Rafuse was hired in his mid-twenties and did odd jobs for the Youngs for much of his working life. He owned a pair of oxen, and the Youngs had him clear land and plant vegetable gardens behind the Maternity Home. The Youngs kept half a dozen cows and goats to supply milk for the mothers. John Rafuse also hauled the cow manure and sawdust — fuel for the burners that heated the Home. He was paid $1.50 a day. "It was hard going back then," he recalls, "but they always paid wages on time and made sure the workers received one square meal a day."

John describes Lila as a "lovely woman, who could have fought any legal case herself, she was that smart." Others in the community had become equally fond of her. Eleanor Marriott, owner of a nearby dairy farm, supplied butter to the Youngs for twenty-five cents a pound. "Everyone knew everyone else," she recalls. "We used to get together for singsongs in various homes... and the women would quilt or hook mats. Lila was as nice as could be, friendly and generous. She would do anything for you." Not everyone was impressed. Charles Longley, the Youngs' lawyer in the 1940s, says she could be "cruel and vicious and had no give or take." Some women who stayed at the Home, though too afraid to speak out at the time, had noted similar traits.

Frank Roy Davis, who would one day feel the edge of Lila's anger, suspected from the beginning that there was something phony about Lila and the Ideal Maternity Home. The rumours of a high infant mortality rate, the doctors' accusations of fraud and the high fees all disturbed him. But for years, hampered by inadequate regulations and an unwillingness to proceed until he was on absolutely solid legal and political grounds, he remained in the dark about what exactly went on behind the Home's doors. The case of Eva Nieforth, the sad young woman from Seaforth who died at the Home on January 1936, shed the first light.

Chapter 4

Eva's Misfortune

In the summer of 1935, Eva Margaret Nieforth often found herself spending endless hours alone walking on a secluded shoreline not far from her home on Nova Scotia's eastern shore. Though slender and attractive Eva was a loner and this isolated spot was the one place where she found comfort when nothing else in her troubled world made sense.

From the shoreline, Eva could see the distant outline of the village where she had been born and raised. Seaforth was a tightly knit community located thirty miles from Halifax. It was predominantly Anglican, and Eva was among the most faithful. On her way home she would pass the one-room school she used to attend and St. James Anglican Church, where she worshipped every Sunday. Lately, her prayers were for forgiveness. Eva had committed a dreadful sin: she had become pregnant out of wedlock. She had always wanted children but not this way. In a place as small as Seaforth, an unwed mother was ostracized, her good character lost forever. No one would marry her, because she was "damaged," and it was unlikely that she would ever find work, because no one would recommend her.

Fortunately for Eva, her family was supportive. The daughter of farmers, she was the youngest of four children. Her brothers, Reg and Stan, were bachelors; her sister, Gertrude, married with children. As a child, Eva had been reclusive, not gregarious like Gertrude, perhaps in part because she was partially deaf. At 28, Eva was only too aware that most of her friends were married, and single women her age were often doomed to spinsterhood.

Her future brightened when she met Walter Nieforth, believed by some in the community to be a distant relative. Like Eva, Walter was partially deaf — a childhood ear infection had never been properly treated — but Walter could speak and read lips. He was several years older than Eva and seemed independent and self-assured. But Walter was a drifter who frequently travelled to western Canada; it was rumoured he had a wife there. He did not have a trade or a steady job, and when he was at home in Seaforth he liked to gamble, drink and spend time with Eva. Walter saw in Eva a chance for a new start, after years of disappointment and failure. But when she became pregnant, he grew edgy and distant. He insisted Eva place the baby for adoption and rejected her pleas for marriage.

Eva Nieforth and her baby died at the Ideal Maternity Home in 1936. Her brother Reginald handled the burial alone.

The gossip drove Walter out of Seaforth, to a small farm in the Annapolis Valley. Desperate and confused, Eva followed, living with him as his housekeeper, all the while hoping he would change his mind and let her keep the baby. But nine days before Christmas 1935, Walter bundled Eva into a horse-drawn sleigh for the long, cold journey to the Ideal Maternity Home. "He just wanted to get rid of the baby," recalls 86-year-old Everett Nieforth, an acquaintance of Walter's. "She was such a nice quiet little girl. I thought it was a damn shame the way she was treated."

Eva was seven months pregnant when she made the journey to East Chester. Wretched and weary, she had abandoned all hope of keeping her child when Walter pulled up in front of the Maternity Home. Walter accompanied Eva inside, where she was signed in under an assumed name, part of the Home's promise to protect unwed women from gossip. Walter gave Lila a down payment of $100 towards the delivery and the adoption of the baby, money Walter was hard-pressed to scrape together. Even a steady workingman would have found the price steep; a clerk or factory worker in Halifax was lucky to earn $2,000 annually during the Depression. Walter, with his drinking and gambling habits, had no idea how he would come up with the remaining bill of $100.

He left East Chester that same night and soon afterwards Eva became ill. For six weeks, she lay on a cot in a small room, alone much of the time. A letter to Walter on January 25, 1936, written in blue crayon, revealed her discomfort and that the birth was not far off.

> *As I picked up the paper to my surprise to see that your mother has passed away. I cannot believe it; it's just like a dream to me. I hope you had gone down for the funeral. How I would have loved to seen her. I never thought that was the last good bye when she left that morning to go to Seaforth. I thought I would see her in the summer. Death surely can take you quick. It's gods will that thy will be done.... I am not feeling so good it takes me in the back every once in a while. I think it will soon come on now. I hope the Lord will help me through in the hour of need.*
> *With love from your little girl E.M.N.*
> *I hope to be home with you soon*
> *xxxxxxxxxxx*
> *xxxxxxxxxx*
> *God Bless You*

Three days later, Eva, in unbearable pain, was rushed to the delivery room. That night her baby boy was either stillborn or died shortly after birth. The next day, Eva appeared to be recovering, but within twenty-four hours, her abdominal infection had inflamed. Without antibiotics — not yet available in rural Nova Scotia — Eva did not have a chance. William Young wrote a hasty letter to her parents.

My Dear Mr. And Mrs. Nieforth:
We regret to tell you that your daughter Eva came to this institution needing professional and institutional care. Her case, is, however, very serious and we fear she will not live very long. We would therefore urge that if you wish to see her alive that you come at your first opportunity. It seems that you live a long distance from either a telephone or telegraph station as I tried to get in touch with you each way so am sending this sad news by letter the first train out from here. Regretting keenly to have to convey such a message to you and hoping you can come shortly.
I am,
Faithfully Yours,
Dr. Wm P. Young, Supt.
P.S. We wish to tell you that she received the utmost care while here, and shall continue to work untiringly for her life....
W.P.Y.

William and Lila also wired an urgent message to Walter. He rushed to the Home but found Eva only semiconscious. He wanted to call in a physician from Chester, but William explained that that was unnecessary as he was a doctor. Before leaving the Home, Walter paid the Youngs $20 for the burial of the infant, and another $5 for its shroud.

The Youngs received a letter from the Nieforths asking about their daughter's health. On February 19, nineteen days after Eva's death, Lila Young responded. The maternity-home letterhead included "Mrs. Dr. Young, Obstetrician" printed in the top left corner.

It is with deepest sympathy that I write these lines in answer to your nice letter received this morning, and we hasten to send you the information you desire. Your daughter entered this institution quite early before her confinement in order that she might be constantly under the skilled attention and to avoid travelling in the heart of winter in her condition. She was far from well for some time before her baby was born and repeatedly told me of a feeling she had that she would never live through this experience. Her baby was dead before birth due to her own physical condition.

Now this institution has to its credit a most wonderful record in the eight years it has been established. During that long period of time there have been no adult deaths in it, and your daughter's death occurred on the eve of its eighth birthday. When you stop to consider that during the past two years alone a baby has been born here on an average of every nine days it shows carefulness and skill on the part of its staff. Our efforts to save your daughter were untiring, and in the extreme, it resulted in a great loss of sleep.

She called to Mr. Walter Nieforth who arrived here early enough to be recognized by her and we tried to get you folks by telephone and telegraph, but could not get the message to you so wrote a letter and motored to the adjoining town where there is an afternoon mail, but no reply has been received. After her baby was born, while she was perfectly conscious, your daughter delivered to this institution a written statement regarding her condition in which she said we had done all for her that could be done. Allow me to again assure you of our sympathy in your late bereavement and assuring you that your daughter received the tenderest care possible.

When the news reached Eva's brother Reg, he travelled by horse and sled in the bitter cold to claim the bodies. Eva was buried in the Anglican cemetery in Seaforth with the baby in her arms. Because she had "sinned," she was not placed in the family plot; instead she was buried at the back of the cemetery. No one in the village wanted to be seen digging the grave, so Reg did it alone, weeping silently as he worked.

The death of Eva Nieforth would become the first highly publicized tragedy at the Ideal Maternity Home, but not the last. Soon most aspects of the Youngs' business practices — their treatment of the girls, the fees charged, causes of deaths and burial practices — would be questioned. The authorities believed that with Eva Neiforth's death, they finally had the evidence needed to effectively challenge William and Lila in court.

Reginald Nieforth, Eva's brother

Chapter 5

Manslaughter

On March 4, 1936, just a month after Eva Nieforth's death, Lila and William Young were ordered into court and arraigned on two counts of manslaughter. The charges stated that the Youngs "did unlawfully kill and slay the said Eva Margaret Nieforth and her infant male child." The Youngs spent a few days in jail before being released on bail. With help from Lila's brothers, Robie, the blacksmith, and Frederick, a justice of the peace, William and Lila each posted a bond of $1,500.

The arrests followed an RCMP investigation prompted by the Youngs' application for burial certificates. Provincial Pathologist Dr. Ralph P. Smith performed the autopsies. The weekly *Bridgewater Bulletin* reported on February 5, 1936, that a coroner's jury was to hear Smith's findings into the deaths of a woman and a "male babe" who had died at "an institution near Chester." Smith concluded that the baby had been born alive and that Eva suffered from peritonitis. He suspected that the cause of the infection, common after childbirth and often fatal, was unsterilized instruments. The infection had travelled through Eva's uterus and fallopian tubes and into the peritoneum. As a result, she developed abscesses, experienced severe abdominal pain; then the abscesses ruptured. Eva had suffered a painful death.

A preliminary hearing opened in Chester on the morning of March 11. The burly crown prosecutor, J.G.A. Robertson, KC, of Bridgewater, opened the proceedings by charging that William and Lila had failed to ensure that Eva received adequate care. He submitted that Eva's son had been born alive and that he had the medical evidence to back it up. Three witnesses testified that day: pathologist Smith, nurse Vallence Dexter Murphy and her husband, Aubrey. The pathologist reiterated that he believed the baby had died because of "instrumental interference." The Murphys revealed that the deaths of Eva and her baby had been so distressing that they both resigned from the Home soon afterwards.

RCMP officers and registrar's office clerks also testified during the two-day preliminary hearing, but some of the most curious testimony came on the last day from Walter Nieforth, Eva's "alleged sweetheart." Transcripts from the hearing no longer exist, but newspaper reports of his testimony reveal that Walter, disheveled and despondent, told a packed courtroom that he had arranged for Eva to stay at the Ideal Maternity Home. When he had seen Eva on January 31, he could not tell whether she was conscious. However, before Crown prosecutor Robertson could complete his questioning, the magistrate, without explaining why, cleared the courtroom. Walter's testimony continued in private. After hearing all the evidence, the magistrate waited a week, then officially ordered William and Lila to stand trial on the manslaughter charges.

In March, during the preliminary hearing into Eva's death, another woman died after staying at the Ideal Maternity Home. Constance Hatt, a married woman from Chester Basin, bled to death after childbirth. Her family applied for a burial permit; the RCMP intervened. Their investigation was inappropriate, to say the least. A pathologist removed her body from the casket and stretched it out on a barn door where he performed a crude autopsy, during which he found no unusual circumstances surrounding the death. Hatt's body was then thrust back into the casket in a disorderly manner for burial. The Youngs accused the pathologist of being incompetent and insensitive.

In April, one month before the Nieforth manslaughter trial, there was a report of another baby death at the Home. Details in *The Halifax Mail* were sketchy: "Yesterday an inquest was held into the death of another child at the Sanitarium, but no evidence was taken pending the findings of the provincial pathologist. The body of the child was forwarded to Halifax and the inquest will be resumed on Tuesday, April 7."

The Eva Nieforth manslaughter trial opened in Lunenburg on May 27, 1936, with Mr. Justice John Doull of the Nova Scotia Supreme Court presiding. It lasted only a few days. The courtroom overflowed with people, but only a few of them had known Eva; any acquaintances would have been too embarrassed to attend and preferred to read about the trial in the newspaper. Later, some relatives tried to dissociate themselves altogether by changing the spelling of their surname to "Neiforth" instead of "Nieforth." Older residents of Seaforth recall that the case was such a scandal that anyone with the name Nieforth dreaded visiting Halifax. It was especially difficult for Eva's father, Rufus, who travelled into the city each morning to sell eggs and vegetables.

The first point of business was the report of the Grand Jury that had been reviewing the evidence. The jury ruled in favour of a trial, which started immediately. Lila and William, represented by J.E. Rutledge of Halifax, pleaded not guilty. Crown Prosecutor J.G.A. Robertson based his case on alleged negligence. A key witness, nurse Vallence Dexter Murphy, described Eva Nieforth's condition when she came to the Home and how it had worsened as the days passed. Then she recounted the delivery itself. Neither of the Youngs had worn masks, she recalled, and Lila found it necessary to use instruments that she did not normally use. Vallence described Lila as careful in her work, kind and attentive to the patients.

Pathologist Ralph P. Smith took the stand at ten o'clock the next morning. To the horror of nearly every spectator, he graphically described Eva's son's injuries to the head and "destruction of the brain." The baby's head had been cut across the top from ear to ear, the occipital bone had been broken off, part of the scalp had been torn away, and two frontal bones had been loosened, a clear indication that high forceps had been improperly used. "Water on the brain" might have made the skull soft and easy to puncture, Smith admitted, but there

YOUNG MANSLAUGHTER CASE OPENS AT LUNENBURG

CHESTER COUPLE ON TRIAL

Plead Not Guilty Before Judge Doull

LUNENBURG, May 26—In a packed courtroom presided over by Mr. Justice Doull, Mrs. Aubrey Murphy, a graduate nurse, today testified in the opening session of the trial of Dr. William P. Young and his wife, Lila P. Young, who pleaded not guilty to four charges of manslaughter.

The case originated early in February last when the accused were arrested in East Chester, where they operated the "Life and Health Sanitarium". Charges were laid following the death in the sanitarium of Eva Nieforth of Seaforth, an unmarried woman, and of her male infant.

EMPLOYED BY ACCUSED

Mrs. Murphy, put on the stand this afternoon by Crown Prosecutor J. W. A. Robertson, said that she had been employed by the Youngs since 1933. She detailed the condition of the Nieforth woman on entering the care of the two accused and enlarged on her general health up to the time of delivery, at which she assisted. This was late in January.

Couple Go On Trial

DR. AND MRS. W. P. YOUNG

East Chester couple who went on trial in the Supreme court at Lunenburg yesterday on charges of manslaughter in connection with the death at the Life and Health Sanatorium last January of Eva Nieforth and her infant son.

The Halifax Chronicle, *May 27, 1936.*

was no evidence of this. He did not think that gloved hands could have caused the injuries. Under cross-examination by Rutledge, Smith said that the baby had breathed… although imperfectly. Smith added that neither the mother nor the child had suffered from "social diseases."

Smith's observation about the baby's breathing was crucial to the case. Prosecutor Robertson knew that to win a conviction he had to disprove Lila Young's claim that the fetus was dead before delivery. He had to show that the baby had been alive, if only for a brief time.

That afternoon, doctors Edward K. MacLellan and Harold B. Atlee corroborated Smith's findings. Other key testimony was given by Walter Nieforth, described by one newspaper as the "self-admitted father of the child" and by another as "a distant relative of the Nieforth woman." Walter told the court that on January 31, he had expressed concern to William Young about the seriousness of Eva's condition, and William had assured him that he was a doctor.

J.E. Rutledge launched his defence by calling Lila Young to

the stand. Lila, "pale and wan… composed throughout," went first on the offensive, accusing some members of the medical community of subjecting her and the Ideal Maternity Home to persecution. She then outlined the rigid moral atmosphere at the Home and said that Eva was the first mother to die at the institution, though she had previously taken two women to hospital in Halifax. Lila had suspected from the start that Eva was carrying a dead fetus. She denied using instruments that could have caused the damage described by the pathologist and said the Home did not do surgical work, including abortions. Nothing more could have been done to save Eva's life, she said. Following his wife to the stand, William Young reinforced Lila's testimony. His appearance was brief; some accounts did not even mention him.

Rutledge then produced his own expert witness, Dr. W.D. Forrest, who praised operations at the Ideal Maternity Home and, not surprisingly, stated that the baby had been stillborn. The Youngs had taken every precaution to save Eva Nieforth, he said. Forrest felt that the Maternity Home had a low mortality rate, given the tendency of unwed mothers to attempt abortions and the generally high rate of infant mortality.

Most of the afternoon of day three was taken up by the address to the jury. Rutledge made an "impassioned plea" for the acquittal of William and Lila. Mr. Justice Doull reviewed the facts presented in court and explained particular points of law to the twelve-man jury. The jurors filed out of the courtroom at five o'clock and returned their verdict just twenty minutes later: not guilty on all counts.

"Husband and Wife Win Court Battle — William and Lila Get Off Free," read the headline the next day in *The Halifax Mail*. Newspapers did not speculate on why the Youngs had been acquitted. A coroner's jury, a magistrate heading a preliminary hearing and a grand jury all had found enough evidence to charge William and Lila and put them on trial, but perhaps, in the jury's mind, Eva Nieforth had been the one on trial. Given the social climate of the times and the venue of the trial

— devout, rural Lunenburg County — Lila's passionate testimony, with its high moral tone, may have been more persuasive than the pathologist's expert findings.

Public Health Minister Frank Roy Davis had lost the first round, but at least now he knew more about the Home and the number of births and deaths there. During the trial, Lila had reported that between 1928 and 1935 there had been 148 births and twelve infant deaths, a mortality rate of 8.1 percent. Unable to pinpoint causes of death, Davis could not compare Lila's statistics to his own department's figures, which showed about a 3.5 percent general incidence of stillbirths between 1930 and 1936. Nevertheless, he must have been alarmed. In 1937, he ordered the RCMP to investigate all known deaths at the Ideal Maternity Home. The first investigation focused on June Marion McAuley, who died on July 22, 1938, of influenza at one month and one day old. The undertaker and attending physician was listed as "Mrs. Lila Young, Grad. Obst." This was one case the Youngs would not soon forget — it led to their first criminal conviction.

Chapter 6

Fraud

Daybreak on a Monday in July 1938, handyman Glen Shatford was inside a workshed at the Ideal Maternity Home searching for dynamite to blast away some bedrock on the property when he accidentally knocked over a scrub board resting on an old wash-basin. The sight and smell made him turn away. "There was this little baby staring up at me," he said. "I couldn't believe it."

Glen had seen dead babies before, but he had never expected to find one in the Youngs' shed. There was no sign of injury, so he assumed it had been stillborn. He put the scrub board back in place, returned to work and for the next five days the tiny corpse remained in the shed.

On Friday before sundown, Glen watched as his employer, William Young, wrapped the tiny body in a sheet and placed it in the trunk of the Youngs' blue Ford. William and Glen then drove twelve miles along Highway No. 3 to the blueberry barrens in Fox Point. They stopped at an uncleared section of land adjacent to a Seventh-day Adventist cemetery. Lila Young's family owned the property, and one of her brothers had granted permission to use it as a burial ground.

Glen Shatford, a handyman at the Ideal Maternity Home, buried many of the babies who died there.

On the way to Fox

Point, William said he wanted to handle this burial himself. Glen thought this unusual, as burials were part of his job. Glen earned a dollar a day, and fifty cents extra when he buried an infant. This time Glen gladly stood aside as William tied a handkerchief around his nose and face, opened the trunk of the car and carried the small bundle toward the burial site. He placed the body in a simple wooden butterbox produced by LaHave Creamery in nearby Bridgewater. These boxes, packed with butter and other perishables, arrived at the Maternity Home with the weekly grocery order. The butterbox was twenty-two inches long, ten inches wide and ten inches deep — just the right size for the little corpse.

William dug a shallow grave, placed the butterbox in the hole, and covered it up. He told Glen nothing of how the baby died. "They always announced when a baby was born," he said. "But if it died, there was a lot of secrecy. That Home… I used to call it the secret place."

The baby William Young buried that morning could possibly have been the daughter of Ethel McAuley, a young woman from Saint John, New Brunswick, who went to the Ideal Maternity Home in July 1938. She had become pregnant after having an affair with Cyril Covey, a married man from Halifax. Ethel had met Cyril at a dance in Saint John nearly a year earlier and, after a brief fling, she told him she was pregnant with his child.

Cyril, a sailor on the Lady Hawkins, had no idea that Ethel had given birth to their child when his ship slipped into Pier 28 in Halifax Harbour on August 5, 1938. After disembarking, he was approached by William Young, who asked Cyril to follow him to his car. Cyril squeezed into the front seat with a large woman introduced as Lila Young; a distraught Ethel McAuley was in the back.

Ethel listened quietly as the Youngs explained to Cyril that she had given birth to his baby at the Ideal Maternity Home, but that she could not afford to pay the bill. They said that the baby, June Marion McAuley, was healthy and being cared for at the Home until an adoption could be arranged. William and Lila told Cyril he was responsible for Ethel's board and the adoption fee.

During the encounter, the Youngs drove along the Halifax waterfront. At first they were friendly, but by the time they pulled up in front of the Nova Scotian Hotel, they had toughened their approach, insisting Cyril pay at least the adoption charge of $150. When Cyril said that he did not have the money, Lila shouted, "Well, you had better borrow it from one of your friends on the ship!"

Next they drove towards the Armdale Rotary in west-end Halifax. Cyril repeated that he could not pay, but William became angry and threatened to tell his friends and family about the baby. He said that he would have Cyril arrested and taken to court. A frightened Cyril, who had a wife and two children at home, yielded to the pressure. They drove to Cyril's home, where Lila, William and Ethel waited in the car while Cyril ran inside for a pen and ink. When he returned, Lila wrote out an agreement, in which Cyril promised to pay the $150 fee in installments. He gave the Youngs the first of those payments, $15. Ethel was told to sign a letter releasing Cyril of his responsibilities when he paid the entire bill.

> I Miss Ethel McAuley, hereafter known as the party of the first part do solemnly declare and promise to release Mr. Cyril Covey known as party of the second part from any further financial responsibility for the support, nurture, education or maintenance of the child born to me at the Ideal Maternity Home, East Chester, Nova Scotia, providing he pays the above mentioned Institution the sum of one hundred and fifty dollars ($150) good and lawful money of Canada.
>
> I also hereby remit, release and forever relinquish any claim on the child born to me and will in no way interfere with its adoption, providing the party of the second part meets his obligation to pay the Ideal

> Maternity Home, East Chester, the sum of one hundred and fifty dollars, fifteen of which has already been paid. The said Institution, assuming responsibility for support of the child. In witness whereof I have set my hand this fifth day of Aug. 1938.

The next time Cyril Covey saw the Youngs was in a Halifax courtroom almost a year later. They had been charged with "defrauding Cyril Covey by using false pretence." The crown had laid the charge after the RCMP had come across a number of suspicious receipts during an investigation at the Maternity Home. Cyril was subpoenaed to give evidence at the trial, at which he discovered the Youngs had lied to him. The prosecution said the Youngs had collected $55 from Cyril for the adoption of his child, after the child was deceased. The baby, born on June 21, died on July 22. Two weeks after the death, the Youngs met Cyril's ship to collect money.

In court, the Youngs' lawyer, J.E. Rutledge, suggested it was Ethel who lied to Cyril.

Rutledge: Wasn't it Ethel who told you that the child was still alive?

Cyril Covey: No, I didn't speak two words to Ethel the whole time.

Rutledge: Was it Dr. Young or Mrs. Young who told you that?

Cyril Covey: It was one or the other. I can't say which one.

Rutledge: Might you on a second thought be mistaken about that?

Cyril Covey: I am sure about that.

Rutledge: And the words you say were, they still had the child — did they use such words as that?

Cyril Covey: I had asked them if the child was still with them, and if they had made any effort to have the child adopted. They said they still had the child, and it was well.

Cyril testified that he did not have anything to do with sending Ethel to the Ideal Maternity Home, and he was not even sure if it was his responsibility to make such an arrangement because he didn't believe she was pregnant with his child. Rutledge pursued this.

Rutledge: Do you deny that you are the father of the child?
Cyril Covey: I don't deny it, but I'm not sure.
Rutledge: Did you have sexual intercourse with her?
Cyril Covey: As far as I know.
Rutledge: Did you or did you not?
Cyril Covey: I can't answer… supposing a man is under the influence of liquor… how would he know?
Rutledge: Do you deny that you had sexual intercourse with her?
Cyril Covey: I'm not denying it, and I don't… affirm it.

Rutledge then called Ethel to the stand where she testified that she had no doubt Cyril Covey was the father. When she discovered her pregnancy she contacted the Youngs after seeing their advertisement in a Saint John newspaper. Ethel had arrived at the Maternity Home five days before giving birth. She had wanted to leave the infant there and return home immediately, but the Youngs would not let her leave. She was forced to accompany the Youngs when they went after the father. On the way to Halifax to meet Cyril on August 5, Lila had insisted that Ethel not mention the baby's death.

Lila had promised to release Ethel from the Home once Cyril agreed to pay the bill, but she reneged on her promise, and Ethel had to stay there for another month. "They kept me there against my will," she said. So afraid the Youngs would report her outstanding debt to the police, Ethel did not even attempt to run away. After hearing the evidence, the jury found William and Lila guilty of defrauding Cyril Covey. The Youngs paid a small fine and returned to East Chester — and business as usual.

There are two other well-documented cases of the Youngs pursuing putative fathers. William once sued a Halifax man, Angus Gillis, the father of baby Murray James. When the mother could not pay her $118 bill, the Youngs took Gillis to court. The judge ordered him to pay the bill in addition to legal costs of $25.25. Unable to pay, Gillis was sent to jail.

Henrietta Henry gave birth to a baby in November 1937 but was unable to pay her bill of $139 for room, board and delivery of her baby. The Youngs pursued her husband, Harry. But Harry argued that he and his wife were legally separated when she became pregnant, and he was not responsible for the bill. The Youngs harassed him and finally threatened to drag him into court. The trial was scheduled for April 19, 1938, but fifteen days before the trial, William Young dropped the charge, without saying why.

Coincidentally, Lila's brother Frederick was also in the business of pursuing putative fathers. A justice of the peace in Fox Point, Frederick frequently heard the cases against putative fathers in his own home. He and Ellison Shatford, a storekeeper from nearby Mill Cove, jointly presided over the "open court" hearings. Because of the titillating nature of the proceedings, people crowded into doorways and hallways to witness the spectacles. Like many JPs in Nova Scotia, Frederick did not have any formal legal education, but he was considered a fine upstanding citizen and a good Liberal, and that satisfied the Attorney General. Political appointees were given the power to try cases and to send people to jail, and in Fox Point, men found guilty of failing to provide child support were imprisoned, usually for ten months.

The Cyril Covey fraud case was an extreme example of the lengths the Youngs went to collect outstanding debts. Public Health Minister Frank Roy Davis and his colleagues did not object to the Youngs' going after the fathers — by the late 1930s, the government was also pursuing them. But government officials did not like the Youngs' tactics. William and Lila often threatened to expose the man. "Lila and William were using blackmail," recalls F.R. MacKinnon, a junior Public Health official at the time. "When you think back to the attitude in those days, exposure in one's community was the ultimate threat." Later, when F.R. MacKinnon became established in government, he would play a key role in efforts to control business practices at the Ideal Maternity Home. F.R. MacKinnon would challenge the Youngs in a way that neither Frank Davis nor the authorities had ever done.

"The death-rate was part of the overall problem," said MacKinnon, who joined the Department of Public Health in 1938. "We suspected that these people were dishonest, not only about the death-rate, but also about their relationship with the mothers, the fathers and the adoptive couples." However, not one RCMP officer or one government official, not even F.R. MacKinnon, knew about the disappearance of Faith Lu Tanya Hatt in July 1939.

Chapter 7

Stolen Baby

Violet Hatt Eisenhauer was a teenager attending school in Chester Basin when she first heard about the Ideal Maternity Home and how it was a secret retreat for girls who were in trouble. The only child of Beatrice Lola and Elbert Henry Hatt, Violet was better off than many of her Depression-era girlfriends, whose families had to scrape for food and clothing. She would make extra money spending her summers under the hot sun, picking buckets of blueberries on the barrens behind her parents' home. On a good day, Violet picked twenty quarts, which she could sell for four cents each. In 1935, eighty cents a day was an excellent wage for a fourteen-year-old.

Midway through grade ten, Violet left school, determined to become a famous writer, but her dark eyes and raven hair had caught the attention of a local boy, Sterling Vincent Eisenhauer. By age eighteen, Violet and Sterling were devoted to each other and planning their marriage. Sterling eventually moved into Violet's parents home in Chester Basin. Sterling was badly in need of a job and decided to join the army; he moved to Halifax and became an infantry cook. Soon after, Violet learned she was pregnant. The hand-knit clothes she collected were blue; she wanted a boy.

When her due date grew near, Violet's parents urged her to go to the Grace Maternity hospital in Halifax, an idea that appealed to them because Sterling would be close by. But Violet felt uneasy about being far from home and insisted that when the time came, her parents take her to the Ideal Maternity Home in East Chester. There, at least, she would be treated by a woman. Violet had heard of Lila Young's fine reputation as an obstetrician, and the cost for "board without adoption," $75, seemed manageable.

At three o'clock in the morning on July 6, Violet was still at home when she went into labour. Her father, too nervous to drive, asked a neighbour to rush her to the Maternity Home, where she was taken into a small, sparsely furnished bedroom in the Youngs' residence. Rooms in the Youngs' home were only available to the married women of Chester. William and Lila were keenly aware of the importance of maintaining good relations with the local people. They made sure they received their full attention and that they did not have to mix with the less fortunate, unmarried girls. Those girls boarded in the Maternity Home next door.

Twelve hours after Violet's arrival, regular contractions began. It was then that Violet suddenly realized something was desperately wrong. Lila was not a doctor — or even a nurse. Violet no longer noticed the excruciating pain as a wave of panic overtook her. For two hours, sure that she and the baby would die, she grasped the iron rungs of the headboard, pushing, gasping for air and pushing again. She knew that the baby was in trouble. Suddenly, Lila told her that the umbilical cord was around the baby's neck, that the infant was in distress, but that she did not know what to do. Lila "kneeled beside the bed and began to pray," Violet said. "She wept as she prayed out loud for God to spare my life."

Violet mustered enough strength to shout to a girl in the next room to call Dr. Douglas Zwicker in Chester. "I knew we had to get help. I thought I was going to die there." As the girl ran towards the phone, Lila bolted from her knees and forbade her to make the call.

Then, as if Lila's prayers were answered, William Young appeared at the door. Finally, a doctor, Violet thought. William delivered the baby safely; it had, in fact, been a breech birth.

"He stayed up all night with me," Violet recalls. "He was afraid I was going to bleed to death,"

Violet awoke the following morning feeling weak, but

proud of her precious eight-pound, six-ounce baby girl whom she named Faith Lu Tanya. For the next two weeks, while Violet nursed Faith at the Youngs' home, her parents visited every day. But her own health was deteriorating. Violet had developed an abdominal infection; she felt nauseated and was unable to eat without vomiting. As part of her treatment, Lila placed large, hot lights over Violet's abdomen, but the heat was so intense that it burned several layers of skin. Lila fed her grapes and freshly squeezed orange juice. When Violet could not drink cow's milk, Lila suggested goat's milk, which was more agreeable. By this time, Lila had regained Violet's trust.

Violet Eisenhauer always believed her baby was stolen from her by William and Lila Young and sold.

While recovering, Violet became friends with several girls at the Home who looked to her for advice and sympathy. Most of them had been unable to pay their bills when they arrived at the Home, so they had to work off their debt. They complained to Violet about the chores Lila forced them to do: they had to scrub floors, clean the kitchen, and wash and iron bundles of bedclothes. With thirty to fifty girls in the Home at a time, the work was exhausting.

Virginia, a fair, blue-eyed girl from Yarmouth, became Violet's closest friend. "I remember one morning she came to me and was very upset," Violet said. "She was a big girl, close to having her baby, and her stomach hurt because she had shaken out every mat in the house that morning. That was the kind of work they did even when they were eight and nine months' pregnant."

Violet also remembered a seventeen-year-old named Betty Anne. "She was a pretty girl from Montreal who came from a wealthy family." When Betty Anne became pregnant, her mother sent her to the Maternity Home with strict instructions that she was not to exert herself, as she was used to having a personal maid. Everyone in the Home knew her parents had paid more money so that she could have extra comforts, but the Youngs ignored the agreement, Violet said. Some days Betty Anne worked in the kitchen so long that her hands blistered.

During Violet's confinement, she remembers two men in hats and overcoats, carrying briefcases, visiting the Home. They approached Violet and asked whether she was comfortable; she told them she was well cared for and that the food was acceptable. Other girls informed Violet that the men were investigating conditions at the Home and that they were asking about baby deaths. The men also asked the mothers whether they knew if the Youngs were accepting money for the babies they were adopting out. The girls could only tell them that when couples arrived, Lila escorted the women to the nursery to view the babies, while the men were ushered to the office to discuss financial matters.

A few days later, Virginia came to Violet with disturbing news: a couple from Winnipeg was expressing interest in adopting Faith. They wanted a baby girl, and except for Violet's, all the babies in the nursery were boys. "I didn't think anything of it because I was married," Violet recalled. "My husband and I were keeping our child. That was made very clear." The next day when the couple returned to the Home, Virginia eavesdropped on their conversation with the Youngs. Listening at the keyhole of the office door, Virginia heard Lila say, "That baby isn't up for adoption," before the conversation moved out of earshot.

July 20, 1940 was a night Violet never forgot. Lila came to her room carrying a baby who looked pale and sick. She held the infant in the crook of her arm and said, "Look, your baby is ill. Do you think she will live?" Violet thought that odd and wondered why Lila stayed in the dim light by the door. "She wouldn't bring the baby close to me, and then I decided it wasn't mine. That baby was bigger and older."

The next morning when Violet was supposed to go home, Lila came to her bedside and told her Faith was gone, that she had "taken a fit through the night and died." Still weak from her pelvic infection, Violet turned on her side and pushed with her elbows into a sitting position. With tears streaming and hand trembling, she pleaded to see the body, but Lila refused. She helped Violet lie back, saying firmly, "You're not in any condition to see the baby. You are too ill."

When Sterling and Violet's parents arrived at the Maternity Home, they saw Lila outside in the garden on her knees, praying. They became alarmed and asked if Violet was all right. The Hatts were shocked to learn the baby had died. When the family asked to see the body, Lila said it was in the basement and "in no condition for viewing." Violet's mother asked that the pink dress she had knitted for baby Faith be put on the infant for the funeral. Lila replied that the dress was no longer there — she had put it on a baby girl who had been adopted the previous day.

The family was distraught but had to be strong for Violet. She had been heavily sedated and had fallen into a deep, medicated sleep; the next thing Violet remembers is waking up at home, certain she would never recover from her loss. Sterling coped with the death by helping with the funeral arrangements. He had already paid the Youngs $75, and now he had to pay an additional fee for a casket.

The day of the funeral, Lila brought the tiny casket to Sterling's mother's house where a wake was held. The casket "had been screwed shut," Violet explained. When her father demanded to see the baby, Lila said it had turned black. "I don't care if that baby is black as tar, I want to see it!" Lila calmly replied, "I'm sorry, Mr. Hatt, I'm not going to open that casket." Later, Elbert Hatt told his daughter that Lila was so determined not to let anyone see what was in the box that he would have had to use force to move her aside.

"Faith" was buried under a large birch tree at Lakeview Baptist Cemetery in Chester. The Youngs stood by until every last shovelful of dirt was thrown and until every family member had left. Only a block of wood marked the grave; Violet never knew who had placed it there.

That night Sterling and Elbert stood in the doorway of the Hatt home with lanterns and shovels, determined to go out into the night to dig up the grave and see what was in the box. But Violet's mother became frantic, pleading that it was against the law to tamper with a grave. "She talked them out of it," Violet said. "I wished she had let them go. Then we would have known for sure if my baby was there. I don't think there was anything in that box. I think they stole my baby and sold her. I can't prove it, but I truly believe that's what happened to Faith." The Hatts never reported Faith's "death" to the police. "My mother wouldn't let us go to the law," Violet said. "So we kept it to ourselves."

After the tragic loss, Violet fell into a deep depression and became seriously ill. She was taken to a Halifax hospital, where doctors cured her abdominal infection. When she recovered and returned home, she spoke with some of the girls at the Maternity Home who told her that they had helped Lila prepare the casket for Faith. The girls had been instructed to use satin and other decorations to cover the casket, a wooden butterbox.

Years later, Violet was plagued by the thought that she should have had the grave opened to see for herself whether a baby was buried there. At one point, her family doctor even suggested exhuming the body to help her regain peace of mind, but Violet did not believe she would get the answers she needed. She was certain the Youngs would have been clever enough to put another infant's body in the butterbox.

Violet was nineteen when she lost her baby, and she never fully recovered. The internal injuries caused during the delivery of Faith were so severe that she was never able to bear another child. Sterling died of a brain tumour when he was just thirty-eight, and Violet spent the next twenty-nine years nursing his mother and her own. Fifty-seven years would pass before Violet would begin to unravel the mystery surrounding Faith; fifty-seven long years before the grave where Faith was allegedly buried was finally dug up.

Chapter 8

Suspicious Deaths

Eleanor Marriott, a neighbour of William and Lila's, had often flirted with the idea of adopting one of the "lovely" babies from the Ideal Maternity home. With her daughter fully grown and her husband at sea much of the time, Eleanor was often lonely. When she approached Lila about the adoption possibilities, Lila asked if she would help out by boarding one of the infants instead. Lila explained that she would be looking after a baby who could not be adopted, but she never said why. "I just assumed the mother couldn't afford to keep it at the Maternity Home because of the expense," Eleanor said. The Youngs charged $300 to board a baby at the Home "for the rest of its natural life."

Eleanor agreed to the boarding arrangement and decided to charge $3 a week to feed, clothe and care for the infant indefinitely. When the baby was brought to Eleanor's home by the young mother one morning, she thought he was adorable, no more than a month old. The older man with them paid Eleanor the $3 for the first week. After the couple left, and Eleanor disrobed the infant to examine him, she was shocked. "He reminded me of a skinned rabbit, so skinny, and his legs so thin."

Eleanor was so alarmed over the baby's condition that she immediately called Dr. Edward K. Woodwoofe in nearby Chester. After examining the infant, Dr. Woodroofe gave Eleanor the bad news: he thought the baby was dying. Eleanor was devastated. She tried to feed the infant milk, but he would only drink a small amount. He did not cry, he whimpered, and before week's end he died in his sleep.

"He died from neglect," Eleanor said sadly. "The doctor said he had not been properly fed. He was terribly malnourished and that's why he died."

After the baby's death a friend of Eleanor's who had worked in the Maternity Home kitchen told Eleanor it was common practice to let the sick or unadoptable babies go hungry. She explained that Lila had instructed the kitchen staff to feed those infants only molasses and water. This would give the infants a small amount of iron, sugar and water but they would go without the vitamins and minerals necessary for survival. On a diet of molasses and water, a baby would starve to death within a few weeks.

To the Youngs, unadoptable babies were those who had any physical defects or birthmarks. They also rejected babies who were not white. If they were bi-racial, aboriginal or black they would not be put up for adoption, a horrible thought considering the large black population in and around the Halifax-Dartmouth area. The kitchen worker, who never reported the feeding system to the authorities for fear of losing her job, said the Youngs would have thought it bad for business to have sick or disabled babies in the Home while couples were arriving to adopt healthy ones. The more cruel reality may have been that with $300 in the Young's pocket, the shorter a child's "natural life," the better.

Angry and distraught, Eleanor attempted to arrange a burial for the baby, but she soon learned that would be impossible. The local undertaker told her he couldn't obtain a death certificate or a burial permit because the child was from the Youngs' Home. The infant's mother was contacted and she came to retrieve the body. Months later, Eleanor received a letter explaining that the baby had been properly buried in the family plot in Mahone Bay. As far as Eleanor knew, no one had ever notified the authorities about the death. After that incident, Eleanor decided to have no further contact with Lila Young, and she shuddered every time she thought of what was happening to the babies inside the Home. "How anyone could do such things, I don't know. Greed is all I can assume."

Eleanor remained suspicious of the business, wondering what people would find if they ever dug up the yard behind the Home. "I heard they had been burying babies there after dark, but I don't think anyone ever proved it." Eleanor recalled that late at night a "peculiar burning smell" emanated from the property. "We would be coming home from the theatre, around 11:30, I guess, and we would notice the smell. We never saw a fire or anything burning, but it always seemed so strange to us."

Stella Mulgrave of Chester Basin, a former employee of the Home, also recalled the burning smell. She had worked for the Youngs for close to a year in the early 1940s when, one night, she opened a door to the basement furnace and saw the partially burned corpse of an infant. Horrified, she ran from the Home and never returned. Stella claims to have reported the incident to the Chester RCMP, but no record of the report can be found. Later, Stella said she never liked working at the Home because she resented Lila's treatment of the babies. Most offensive, she said, was Lila's habit of referring to them as "little bastards."

The starvation of the infants was just an inkling of what was really going on at the Ideal Maternity Home. Glen Shatford, the handyman who found a body in the Youngs' workshed, had worked at the Home for about a year. "I know for sure there were 100 to 125 babies buried there in the 1930s," he said. "We buried them in rows, so it was easy to see how many there were." Glen buried some of the babies, as did handyman George Westhaver, Lila's brother Murray Coolen and the Youngs themselves. "I remember burying at least five or six of them by myself, possibly more," Glen admitted. "If butterboxes were not available, the workmen made crates, a few pieces of board nailed together and Lila put a shroud on the corpse. Sometimes she said a hurried prayer at the gravesite, especially when people were within earshot."

During one burial Glen was just about to cover the grave

when Lila spotted someone approaching in the distance. "She dropped to her knees and started praying. It was a sight," Glen said with a chuckle. "The words poured out. I just stood there and waited. I liked her, but she was an awful bull-shitter. Blarney mouth, that's what I used to call her." The Youngs would not permit burials on the "seventh day," between sundown Friday and sundown Saturday, so if a baby died during that time it wouldn't be buried until the following week, when the handymen returned to work.

Anna MacKenna, a Cape Breton woman who had a baby boy at the Home in the mid-1940s, was there when a baby died. When she asked Lila about a funeral, Lila said, "Oh no, we don't do that." She then wrapped the body, took it out the back door of the Home and left it on the steps. The next morning, Anna looked out and the baby was gone. Presumably one of the handymen had buried it.

The number of infant deaths at the Home presumably increased with the volume of business, but without autopsies it can never be known how most of the babies died. Glen Shatford assumed many had been stillborn. Cecil Coolen, Lila's brother, recalls that the men who worked there said some girls were so desperate they douched with turpentine in an attempt to abort the child. He wondered if that was why so many were deformed.

Violet Hatt Eisenhauer knows of at least one baby that died from neglect. In 1939, when Violet was at the Youngs' residence delivering her baby, she and her friend Virginia were bedridden when they heard a baby scampering across the floor in another room. Violet screamed, "I think that baby is near the stairway." Next, they heard a loud thumping. The baby had fallen down the stairs, screeched and fell silent. Lila Young and the girls were next door in the sanitarium for daily prayers at the time.

Whispers about what was going inside the Ideal Maternity Home grew louder when people began to hear about babies buried at sea. Eleanor Marriott, the woman who had once boarded a Maternity Home infant, admitted years later that her husband had been paid to dump some of the tiny bodies from his fishing boat, sometimes twice a week.

But if the local people knew a lot, they reported very little. One reason was that, locally, the Youngs had become a powerful economic force during hard times. Ray Corkum lived most of his life near the Youngs. He was a boy when his father, Edward, a storeowner and lumberman, became friends with Lila and William. Edward sold the Youngs lumber when they expanded the Home and groceries from his store, Corkum and Mader's General, in Chester. "They were the finest people you would ever want to meet," Ray recalled. "Their ability to throw around money and pay cash for goods during the Hungry Thirties was a luxury. Just think, 50 to 75 girls to feed, all those babies, and the Youngs' family, too. In a little place like East Chester, that was a great deal of money."

Nonetheless, the Youngs became increasingly controversial by the late 1930s and, as a result, were taking steps to protect themselves legally. They attached a waiver to their "power of attorney" contract. Each girl absolved the Ideal Maternity Home of any responsibility for the death of her child and gave the Youngs the right to bury the infant "according to the usually adhered to custom." This sample contract from the 1940s also shows that the fees for burial — $20 in the early years — had increased.

> I fully realize the uncertainty of life anywhere especially with babies, and I hereby express my confidence in the Staff of the said Ideal Maternity Home and Sanitarium Limited to do all for the babies entrusted to their care, but should in the Providence of God that my said child should die while in the custody of the said institution, the management shall make all arrangements for the burial of the said child in a Christian manner according to the usually adhered to custom, and place of burial, for which service I agree to promptly pay the sum of thirty-five dollars.

The Youngs' activities outside of the Maternity Home became increasingly bizarre during this period. In 1938, they were "disfellowshipped" by the Seventh-day Adventist Church. The church gave no reasons for expelling the Youngs, but half a century later, after stories about the Maternity Home had aired on television, the Seventh-day Adventists were asked to comment on the case. An ambiguous press release stated that through "practice and behaviour" the Youngs had violated the fundamental teachings of the church, and the "disregard for life, and the sale of life would place a member's standing... under review." The church did not elaborate.

The statement is the only official reference made by the church to the Youngs' involvement in baby selling. Outwardly undaunted by their dismissal, and to save face, William and Lila told friends and acquaintances they had left the church voluntarily because "the girls needed us more." The Youngs immediately joined a marginal sect, the Evangelical Church, begun in 1937 by Bishop Clifford Morash. Wearing a Homburg and a long black coat, he travelled along the South Shore holding Evangelical services. The Evangelical Church itself was a one-room wooden building with cathedral-like windows located a stone's throw from the Maternity Home.

Morash, a native of East Chester, had spent time in a United Stares prison for defrauding war widows. "I was converted in prison," he would cry. "I have been saved." To most, Morash's behaviour and advice were highly suspect, but William and Lila liked what he stood for. "Don't you swallow any pills," he would warn. "And stay away from those doctors. If you get sick, that is the Lord's will."

Morash had only a dozen followers when Lila and William joined, but they stayed with the Evangelical Church throughout the 1940s. Morash baptized their eldest son, William, and buried five babies from the Ideal Maternity Home.

Part II

Dangerous Fixation
1939–1945

Chapter 9

Mounting Suspicion

By 1939, Canada was pulling itself out of the deprivation of the Depression and preparing to send its young people to war. Halifax, whose economy always peaked during wartime, was a major disembarkation port for the troops. Canadian and foreign warships crowded into the harbour, and the downtown streets were scattered with service personnel. Suddenly, people had far more to worry about than a home for unwed mothers.

Because of the population boom, the city's social services were stretched to the limits. The Nova Scotia Children's Aid Society's two social workers had their hands full controlling street trades — youngsters as young as seven were selling newspapers late at night and begging in order to support their poverty-stricken families. The workers also made efforts to curb parental neglect and to counsel "cruel and neglectful" foster parents. The 183 unmarried mothers known to the Society in 1939, for the most part, stayed in city-based homes affiliated with the church and government. Private maternity homes, out of sight and reach of the social workers, continued unregulated.

Lila and William's good fortune began to sour when F.R. MacKinnon, a bright and ambitious twenty-eight-year-old, returned to Nova Scotia in 1940 after spending a year in Chicago studying new adoption procedures and child-welfare laws. "When I began in public health, I had definite plans to see the introduction of new adoption laws, and standing directly in my path, sticking out like a sore thumb, was that Home," MacKinnon said.

In Chicago, MacKinnon had learned that Nova Scotia

adoption laws were grossly inferior to those of other jurisdictions. In 1939, for example, Great Britain had passed a law prohibiting the advertisement of babies for adoption. In other provinces and certain states, the government required maternity homes to be licensed. Moreover, government employees had to approve every adoption, and there were waiting periods from one month to a year before adoptions were finalized. In addition, psychiatric evaluations of adoptive couples were conducted, and follow-up home inspections were carried out.

Nova Scotia's Director of Child Welfare, F.R. MacKinnon, spent years trying to prove the Youngs were selling babies.

F.R. MacKinnon knew that William and Lila's freedom to maneuver was enhanced by impotent legislation in Nova Scotia. The few child-welfare laws that did exist were narrow in scope and usually not enforced. The adoption laws of 1896 required consent from the natural mother, but the rule was waived if an infant had been supported by a charitable institution, incorporated by law, for two years prior to the adoption petition. The Infants' Boarding House Act of 1897 required licences from the municipalities in which the homes were located, but it was rarely enforced. MacKinnon thought that those laws still in effect in the 1930s were "from the dark ages; they were Neanderthal. No one really cared about the mothers or their babies." Certainly William and Lila benefited from government leniency; in their first twelve years in business they never once obtained a licence, and no one had objected.

Because of the education he received in Chicago, MacKinnon was appointed Assistant Director of Child Welfare, and he soon became eager to play an active role in reforming

Nova Scotia laws. By the time he returned to Halifax, Dr. Frank Davis was drafting a law requiring private maternity homes to be licensed by the Department of Public Health. Davis was responding to pressure from the Children's Aid Society, which argued that private maternity homes were "known to exploit the unmarried mother and provided poor standards of care." Davis and MacKinnon also had their own reasons for wanting laws that gave them greater control. Through newspaper advertising and brochures, the adoption business was becoming highly profitable; Lila and William Young, and other private maternity homeowners, were cashing in. On and off throughout the first three months of 1940, the Halifax *Chronicle* ran the following ad:

> Home for unmarried mothers. No Publicity. Infants have complete adoption service. Maternity specialist. Rates reasonable. Write for information: Ideal Maternity Home, East Chester, Nova Scotia.

At least one other privately run business was in competition with the East Chester home. The following ad appeared under Special Notices in the Halifax *Chronicle* during the same three months.

> PRIVATE MATERNITY HOME
> by graduate nurse. Adoption service.
> B-1047. Box 284 Chronicle.

Such flagrant publicity roused the ire of both Davis and MacKinnon; they inspected the homes but were unable to find any evidence of baby trafficking, a business morally frowned upon but not illegal. They learned that the Youngs had been receiving calls from lawyers in the United States and Canada who had clients wanting to adopt, and that the Youngs were mailing these lawyers advertising brochures and postcards. They were not able to establish an exchange of money for babies. "We knew they were selling babies," MacKinnon said later, "but we couldn't find a shred of evidence. Nobody would talk." MacKinnon recalls that the Youngs' baby selling practice was common knowledge in the community. "Everyone around there had heard about that end of the business," he said, "but our actions were based on suspicion only. We could not prove anything."

Many in the community could not imagine how two people doing so much to help troubled girls could sell their infants. Others who knew about the business simply chose to keep quiet. Without solid evidence, Davis, the more politically vulnerable of the two, decided not to act impetuously, at least in part not to alienate his constituents. Many business people appreciated and supported the Youngs and were convinced that a service for pregnant girls was necessary. Some probably had a sincere interest in a home for the poor and disadvantaged, but others knew that the Home was increasingly protecting daughters of the rich. As the business grew, so did stories about the well-to-do who had slipped up. Rumours that Lila Young was conducting illegal abortions for the elite of Halifax began surfacing. Lila had always insisted that she conducted no such operations at the Ideal Maternity Home. Throughout the years, she maintained that the only abortions she knew of were attempted before the girls arrived at her home. Government inspectors tried but were unable to prove her wrong.

Lila was furious at government efforts to control the Home, after it had been operating independently for twelve years. She told anyone who would listen that Frank Davis and F.R. MacKinnon were picking on her. She was so vocal that she created a public debate about the proposal to licence maternity homes. Business people in the community took sides. Some, including her eldest brother, Frederick, made it clear to Frank Davis that he or any other officious bureaucrats harassing these "legitimate" entrepreneurs was not welcome. "That was why Davis blew hot and cold," F.R. MacKinnon explained. "Politically, he was responding to the community, and a large number of people thought he was out of line trying to control the adoption business. As a politician, he was merely representing the people."

It might seem surprising that a lone businesswoman operating in rural Nova Scotia could be a constant thorn in the side of a powerful cabinet minister, but in her own territory Lila Young was also powerful. She had brought new money to an area where there was none, and the people indebted to her would remain loyal. But Lila's territory was also Davis's territory. Because Chester and East Chester were in his constituency, he relied heavily on support from the local doctors, shopkeepers and other community leaders. These were the people who had helped elect him. As a politician, he had to tread lightly.

While crafting the new licensing requirements, Davis and MacKinnon began more regular and more thorough inspections at maternity homes throughout the province. MacKinnon, who usually conducted the inspections, visited the Halifax Infants' Home and other private institutions in Halifax once or twice a year. He found them cooperative and compliant. It was more difficult getting to homes outside the city because transportation was slow and the winters severe. A visit to a facility outside Halifax took all day. As a result, the few rural homes were not inspected as often as they should have been.

But growing suspicion of irregularities prompted F.R. MacKinnon to make an exception and drop by the Youngs' Home two or three times a year. The inspections were usually unannounced and always tense. "When we arrived we would be sermonized by both of them," MacKinnon recalls." We would be told what marvelous things they were doing for the girls. At the same time they would attempt to make us feel inadequate and guilty because of the deficiencies in our own structure."

Those deficiencies, according to critics such as Lila, related to inadequate moral and financial support for unmarried mothers. The government, while thwarting women's efforts to give up their babies for adoption, was not providing support to girls at privately run homes. Frank Davis, like most of his contemporaries, held harsh views of these "troubled" girls; they had created their problems, so they should resolve them.

While being "sermonized," F.R. MacKinnon walked through the nursery, interviewed some of the girls, looked at financial statements and spoke with William and Lila. By 1941–42, the Home had more than one nursery, with an average of seventy infants at any time, ranging in age from a few days to three years old. "I looked at the babies to see if they were well cared for, but remember, I was a social worker, not a doctor or nurse, so I wouldn't have had the training to look at them from a medical point of view. I could not assess the adequacy of the delivery room or sterility of the instruments, for example, so I looked at the Home from a social point of view."

It would be years before a medical expert would be on hand for inspections, an indication of how apathetic the government really was when it came to the treatment of unwed mothers and their babies. When informed of the fee schedule, F.R. MacKinnon became immediately suspicious. "It lent itself to abuses," he said later. "With an up-front lump-sum payment system, there would have been an incentive to move the girls in and out quickly. The faster they got rid of them, the more money they would make." He advocated a *per diem* system, which would have been fairer to the prospective mothers. Paying by the day would at least have given them a chance of receiving proper care.

Initially, when it looked as if F.R. MacKinnon might be easily influenced, Lila was friendly, but when it became clear that he had a critical eye, she became annoyed and impatient. "Let's face it," MacKinnon said. "On the surface the inspections didn't tell us a hell of a lot. It was the discussions with Mr. and Mrs. Young where we gathered our information and made assessments. That was where we could determine if someone was trying to put one over on us."

After very few discussions, MacKinnon grew wary and distrustful of the business. For Lila and William Young he developed an intense disdain. They were "too obsequious, too oily and too preachy. They registered as phonies five minutes after I met them. They had this religious front, and religion was coming out of every pore, oozing out of every gland, it could make you sick."

During one visit, William, who naively did not see MacKinnon as a threat, told him about a couple who wanted to adopt twins. He explained to MacKinnon that he did not have any, but that he would simply pair up two babies and pretend they were twins. The adopting couple, William said, would never know the difference. "I was appalled," MacKinnon remembers. "He would have doctored the birth certificates and claimed they were authentic twins. And he didn't think there was anything wrong with that, ethically or morally!"

MacKinnon thought there should have been an on-staff medical doctor. But Lila usually sidestepped that issue by explaining that she had a doctor on call and did not need a resident physician. Lila was confident that she could handle any deliveries herself. MacKinnon remembers Lila saying she knew more about delivering babies than any doctor. Charles Longley, too, was convinced Lila could do the job. "She knew all about difficult deliveries; but not William... I don't think he could have handled it." Clearly, Longley was unaware of the night Lila had fallen to her knees in prayer when she thought she would lose Violet Eisenhauer and her baby.

Lila's family in Fox Point knew of her reluctance to hire a doctor. Her youngest brother, Cecil, once talked to Lila about it. "Frank Davis actually offered to work with Lila. She told me that herself," Cecil said. "Davis said if she hired a doctor to deliver the babies, he would make certain that babies went into good homes. She didn't accept the offer, though; I don't know why. I guess it would have cut into her profits."

There were only two qualified doctors in the Chester area, Douglas Zwicker and Edward K. Woodroofe; both refused to be on call for the Home. They did not approve of Lila and were still upset that she and William were pretending to be doctors. In the mid-1940s, former Chester Board of Trade President Phil H. Moore wrote to the local newspaper supporting a proposal to have a resident doctor at the Home, although, he said, doctors who live nearby are always on call. Dr. Woodroofe answered promptly in a letter to the editor. "As a doctor who does live nearby, I wish to state that I am definitely not on call to the Ideal Maternity Home. And that in the ten years that I have lived in Chester, I have never set foot in that Institution."

If adoptive couples insisted on medical check-ups for the babies, Lila referred them to a Halifax pediatrician, Barrie Coward. In the beginning, Dr. Coward did not ask too many questions, and he did not follow up after the babies were taken from his office. Unlike the doctors in the Chester area, Dr. Coward was not prepared to interfere in the Youngs' adoption business.

In 1933, when Dr. Coward opened his office on Robie Street in Halifax, he was the only certified pediatrician in the province. In the early years, he examined only a few babies from the Ideal Maternity Home. By the 1940s, when his reputation as a pediatrician was well established, his services were used more often, perhaps a dozen times a year. "The adoptive parents wanted me to see the child and pass an opinion as to whether it would be safe to adopt," Dr. Coward recalled. "They wanted to know whether the infant would grow into a healthy, normal child. I think a lot of them used to think we could tell whether their baby was going to be an Einstein or a Beethoven or someone of that sort, but of course we couldn't."

Dr. Coward conducted basic examinations of the infant's eyes, ears, nose and throat. He did not have sophisticated methods for checking the heart, lungs and central nervous system, but he did what he could. He had various methods for determining whether the infant was mentally fit. "I tested the infant's reflexes and response to sounds and quick movements to see if he or she reacted in a normal way. I would watch for expressions on his face and hold something in front of him to see if he reached for it — various tests." Assessing the emotional state of the infant was most difficult, Dr. Coward told the adopting parents. He felt that much of the emotional development depended on environment and the maternal care and affection given the child. "A lot of these babies from the Ideal Maternity Home were put in their beds and left there. They weren't played with and not stimulated the way they would have been in a private home. I would take that into consideration."

Dr. Coward explained that babies from the Home frequently suffered from colds and ear infections but, he told couples, these ailments would likely disappear once the infants were in a better environment. "In a nursery the contact level was high and infections swept through, particularly with babies whose resistance was already low." He recalled a number of occasions when he advised couples not to adopt a particular infant because of deafness or some other disability. "Unless they were very attached to that particular baby, I would advise against the adoption," Dr. Coward said. "Normally, I would not hear back from the couple, so I would never know if they kept the infant or returned it to the Ideal Maternity Home. I never did know what happened to those babies."

Dr. Coward did not keep records for the Home infants he examined because they were not regular patients. "It was not like families coming in once a year for check-ups," Dr. Coward explained. "These were incidental cases, where couples came in once for a so-called expert opinion. They came and they went. I saw no need to keep files on these patients."

Dr. Coward did not have extensive personal dealings with William or Lila; however, he eventually became irritated over their adoption business. Removing a baby from the province without proper scrutiny by social workers upset him. "I was concerned for the children. So many couples would come to see these babies, pick one they liked… and take it. They wouldn't think of having the baby examined medically, and no one seemed to be monitoring the adoption process. It just wasn't right." Dr. Coward might have felt strongly about the poor monitoring system, but several years would pass before he joined government forces in their condemnation of practices at the Ideal Maternity Home.

No one complained when Patricia Ann, adopted by Annie Boutilier of nearby Marriott's Cove, was taken from the Home without being examined by a doctor. Annie, a friend of Lila's, was a respected, middle-aged married woman who had raised four children of her own. When they were grown, she became lonely and often talked about adopting a baby. Eventually, Annie became serious about the adoption and browsed through the nursery several times before selecting eleven-month-old Patricia. Because Annie was Lila's friend, and related to R. Clifford Levy, who later became the Youngs' lawyer, it was unlikely she had to pay for the baby.

Patricia appeared healthy except for her skin, which was red and blistering because she had been left in wet diapers too long. Once when Annie visited the Home, she counted twenty-two babies and only one girl to care for them. Patricia, later renamed Kathleen, was born in June 1943. It was not until she was almost six years old and preparing to start school that a doctor discovered she was partially deaf. Hearing aids were not available, so with the help of her mother and friends from New Jersey who spent summers in Marriott's Cove, Kathleen learned to read lips. Although her speech was not perfect, she began school when she was eight. "My mother didn't think Lila had known about my hearing problem when I was a baby," Kathleen explained later. "It was something no one could have known about… I guess."

However, like Barrie Coward, F.R. MacKinnon thought doctors or child-care workers ought to have known the condition of babies such as Patricia, who had come from the Ideal Maternity Home. In April 1940, the Maternity Boarding House Act, requiring maternity homes to have licences from the Nova Scotia government, was introduced in the legislature; it came into effect that September. Under the new law, institutions such as the Ideal Maternity Home had to maintain a register containing the names, ages, and addresses of girls checking in, to be sent to the Director of Child Welfare. Homes had to be open for inspection at all times, and advertising for the adoption of children under three years of age was prohibited. In an effort to obtain an accurate reading on mortality at the homes, the law required that the Director of Child Welfare be notified within twenty-four hours of the death of a mother or baby. Persons failing to report a death or violating any other section of the law would have to pay a fine not exceeding $100 or spend up to thirty days in jail.

Lila and William had to either comply with the regulations or close down. They chose to comply, to a point. They made certain the girls' names were inscribed in a register and reluctantly sent copies to the Public Health Department. They began reporting deaths to the Child Welfare Director and gave assurances they would no longer advertise babies for adoption. As a result, the government issued the Ideal Maternity Home a licence in 1941. William and Lila could now reassure people the Nova Scotia government approved of their business practices. In their brochure they wrote:

> The latest model of automatic steam-heated AutoClave Sterilizers are used in the work, and its staff is guided by a modernly equipped laboratory for the safety of all, as well as other modern equipment, and the institution is licensed by the Government of Nova Scotia to conduct the work as outlined in this little booklet.

Issuing the licence created friction within the government. F.R. MacKinnon, who had deepening doubts about the Youngs' intentions to live up to the requirements, felt the licence should have been denied. However, Frank Davis, conscious of public opinion favouring the Youngs, made a political decision. "It was decided it was better to try to work with them and have some control over their business rather than having them unlicensed and have no control," MacKinnon conceded later. He realized his distain for the Youngs and his suspicions of unethical business practices had to be suppressed until he had proof.

Chapter 10

Baby Barons

As it did for so many marginal businesses, the war turned the Ideal Maternity Home into a flourishing factory; wartime produced an illegitimate-baby boom. Sailors, about to ship out or returning after horrific dangers and tragic losses at sea, sought pleasure with a vengeance. The Ajax Club and other dance halls were overflowing with servicemen and their sweethearts. Illegitimate births throughout the province soared by nearly fifty percent.

Many women with unwanted babies took advantage of the discreet adoption arrangement at the East Chester maternity home. Their bills were often paid by servicemen out of their fat wartime wages. Handyman John Rafuse remembered a steady stream of girls arriving at the Home. When they finished their assigned tasks — washing dishes, laundry and looking after babies — they knitted socks and sweaters for the men fighting overseas. Lila encouraged such activity; after all, she had a vested interest in keeping the home fires burning. "Lila didn't knit," Rafuse said, "just the girls did. Lila was too busy running the business."

As the flow of business increased, so did the cost of staying at the Home. The privacy girls had paid for in the 1930s was even dearer in the 1940s: a minimum of $300 for the delivery and adoption of babies. Despite the high cost, many still chose East Chester over the more judgmental church-run institutions such as the Home of the Guardian Angel, the Halifax Infants' Home, the Little Flower Institute in Little Bras D'Or and the Salvation Army Girls' Home in Sydney.

Discretion remained the main attraction at the Ideal

Maternity Home, but the sales pitch was changing. William and Lila had become more publicly religious, adding Christian forgiveness to their promises of confidentiality. F.R. MacKinnon saw William and Lila as religious charlatans. "Both Mr. and Mrs. Young claimed to be part of a religious organization that was very fundamental, strict by the Bible. Their approach was appealing, and people thought these God-fearing, godly people could not possibly be wrong."

The Youngs' lawyer at the time, Charles Longley, was also uncomfortable with the religious pitch. "When I was around, she quoted the scripture from morning till night. It was 'God bless you' and 'the Lord be with you' every time she opened her mouth. I could hardly stand it." The Youngs' increasingly sanctimonious approach was evident in their new brochures:

> All through the ages babies have been born out of wedlock, and every thinking person KNOWS the same condition will continue. Some people have the idea that such a condition can be suppressed by punishment; others seem to get enjoyment from gossip when a young woman is seduced but when a similar condition was brought to Christ, as recorded in the Bible, there was a striking example for us to follow. As Christ gazed into the faces of men who brought the woman to him taken in adultery, He read the sins of their wicked lives and said: "Let him that is without sin cast the first stone at her." Then he simply stooped down and wrote on the sand words that caused one after another of her accusers to sneak away in disgrace. Then with her accusers gone, the only one without sin said, "neither do I condemn thee; go and sin no more." Dame gossip has sent many young lives to perdition after ruining them socially, they might have been BRIGHT STARS in society and POWER in the world of usefulness, had they been shielded from gossip when they made a mistake.

One well-to-do family in Saint John, New Brunswick, was more than willing to pay for the privacy at the Ideal Maternity Home. In 1943, Kate Davidson, twenty-four, was planning her wedding when she found out she was pregnant. Soon after, her fiancé, a Royal Air Force pilot, was killed. She confided in her father, who, after seeing an advertisement in the classified section of the local newspaper, sent Kate to East Chester.

In April 1944, Kate gave birth to a girl, healthy in every respect except for a small tumour on her lip. But it was enough to make adoption difficult. Kate returned to Saint John, but could not get over the separation from her baby. Three years later, in 1947, she did get married and when she told her husband about her illegitimate child, he agreed to help search for her. But when they returned to the Maternity Home, Lila told them the baby had died. Kate was convinced the death was punishment for her sin. Forty years would pass before she learned that her daughter was alive and well and had been adopted by a family in Timberlea, a small community on the outskirts of Halifax.

William and Lila bent the truth when convenient, but there was one promise they faithfully kept: secrecy. Edward Brownell, a former head of Parent Finders, an agency that helps adoptees find their birth parents, witnessed 150 reunions between mothers and children, but only three involved children from the Ideal Maternity Home. "They did their job well," Brownell says, "taking extreme measures to submerge the identities of the birth mothers."

For many years Brownell kept Ideal Maternity Home brochures that urged the girls to enter the Home early to avoid "gossip," and to get away from acquaintances before they could learn that a baby was expected. "Wise girls enter our refuge months before baby is born to safeguard their future, which might be ruined otherwise. A word to the wise is sufficient."

Business was brisk in the fall of 1944, when a young Nova Scotian woman wrote to the Youngs asking for information about their services. The reply was sent by William Young, "vice-president" of the Maternity Home. He outlined the service offered, the cost and the importance of making reservations early:

> *Since our bookings are extremely heavy, it will help if you will send us the enclosed card for your reservation as early as possible. Above all, do not leave your coming too late, because so many babies are born premature and your entire future might be endangered by delay... For the sake of the unborn and for your own comfort, we want you to enter this institution free from worry and care so you can enter into the happy spirit of the place. The best way to accomplish this is to have all financial matters provided for before you enter. Assuring you of our utmost care and a warm welcome upon your arrival.*

The registration form that accompanied William's letter, like the Home's contracts, was professionally produced, elaborate and detailed. Registrants were asked for the physical descriptions of the birth mothers and fathers — height, weight, age and colour of eyes — as well as the religion, education, nationality and racial origin of the parents. They were even asked about musical abilities. There were other questions about family history: Do you come from a long-lived family? Parents' names and address? Do they know your secret? Who is financially responsible?

The "transfer agreement" stated that apart from the $300 charge for delivery and adoption, girls had to pay $20 for a layette and $50 if the transfer payment was to be made more than two weeks after the birth. All girls signed the following statement:

> IN HARMONY WITH the current price list quoted above, I hereby enter into this registration contract with the Ideal Maternity Home and Sanitarium Limited At East Chester, Nova Scotia, of my own free will and accord, willingly and cheerfully submitting to the rules and restrictions prescribed by its staff. I fully realize that

> this is an obstetrical hospital and not a mere boarding house, and that the object of my coming here is for the purpose of being confined. I therefore contract hereby for my complete care, during, before, and after confinement until fully recovered from confinement effects. In witness whereof I hereunto set my hand and seal at East Chester, Nova Scotia.

The contracts, though never challenged in court, probably would not have been legally binding for girls under the age of majority. But the many uneducated, vulnerable girls who went to the Home for help believed the contracts legally bound them to submit to the Youngs' demands.

Clearly William and Lila were receiving legal advice on how to protect themselves if Frank Davis or anyone else challenged their rules and regulations. By this time, the detailed family histories needed to satisfy couples wanting to adopt were also required by most of the church-run maternity homes.

With the guaranteed privacy pitch of the East Chester Home, the supply of babies increased. During the early 1940s, more than a hundred babies were crammed into the Home's hot, congested nurseries at any one time. Their bassinets, with a nametag on each, were lined up, row after row, boys on one side, girls on the other. A steady flow of childless couples, eager to adopt, moved through the nurseries, examining the babies. One parent later said it was like shopping at a Safeway store.

As couples passed through the door into the institution, they were handed the Youngs' ever-present brochures:

> Babies born in this institution are given a scientific start in life and a foundation upon which to build. Special equipment is provided for the development of the delicate babies under the direction of a baby specialist. Then to that large class of young mothers who realize fully their inability to provide the many and costly advantages to her child that can be lavished

upon him by foster parents, we offer a COMPLETE ADOPTION SERVICE.

Lawyer Charles Longley, who handled the Youngs' adoption business throughout the war years, welcomed William and Lila's business. Longley and his brother had opened their law practice in the middle of the Depression, and keeping it afloat had not been easy. Four months after opening, they had earned $8.01. "We took $4 each and left a penny in the till," Longley recalls. Eventually they began handling collection accounts for funeral homes. The money was a bit better, but the work was unpleasant.

Working for the Youngs, the money was good — $165 per case — and Longley was busy. He handled between fifteen and twenty adoptions every month from 1941 to 1946. "In those days, no one was guillotining the Youngs, so we were able to put through a great number of adoptions," he remembers. The demand for Nova Scotia babies developed, in part, because the Ideal Maternity Home was one of the few adoption agencies that did not discriminate against couples because of religion.

Religious discrimination seeped into most aspects of everyday life. Prior to the 1960s, the Halifax Police and Fire Departments, for example, were traditionally seen as employers of Protestants and Catholics. Department veterans remember that when a Catholic retired, a Catholic was hired, and when a Protestant retired, a Protestant was hired. For decades, the election of a Catholic mayor in Halifax had to be alternated with the election of a Protestant mayor. Finally, in 1955, a Jewish candidate, Leonard Kitz, was elected, breaking the pattern.

When it came to adoptions, virtually all government-supported, church-operated homes, as well as the Children's Aid Society, would only place Catholic babies in Catholic homes. The Presbyterian, Anglican and Jewish organizations also prevented adoptions across sectarian lines. With religion playing such a significant role, Jewish couples found it almost impossible to adopt. F.R MacKinnon says that in all his years in government he never once came across a Jewish illegitimate child. Jewish women, raised within a strong religion, were taught that sex belongs within marriage. The teenaged girls led sheltered lives, but if they became pregnant, the pressure to marry was intense. Pregnancy out of wedlock and abortions were matters best kept within the family. Before a Jewish girl "in trouble" had to resort to the public system, she would be looked after by her extended family. An illegitimate baby would be adopted by a relative, normally a grandmother or aunt, or quietly transferred to a larger centre for adoption through Jewish Family and Child Services.

Charles Longley, the Young's lawyer for many years, handled the adoption of hundreds of babies from the Ideal Maternity Home.

If mid-century social values permitted the Youngs to operate with very little scrutiny, religious territorialism positively encouraged them. "The government wanted to match the eyes and the religion of every baby," Charles Longley said. "There were so many silly little details that didn't make a damn bit of difference." The religious policy was not even a law, it was simply a practice, but no one dared violate it. MacKinnon agreed that no one in government would consider placing a Catholic child in a Protestant or Jewish home, even if there was a surplus of babies. "It just wasn't done. Legally it would have been possible, but from a practical or political point of view, any public servant approving that would be courting disaster because inevitably somebody would tell."

Charles Longley suggests that the Ideal Maternity Home was the only institution on the continent that had a surplus of babies who could be placed in homes regardless of religion. Most of those couples for whom he arranged adoptions were Jewish couples from the United States. Longley helped them obtain visas and passports.

Lila Young's absence of religious boundaries put her years ahead of her time, Longley says. "A lot of these children, if left with the welfare department and government, would never have been placed in homes," Longley says. "They would have remained wards of the court and ended up in foster homes, and when they grew older would have become potential criminals. These people took it upon themselves to advertise and drum up business and place them in homes. I always felt that any home was better than no home."

Longley commends the Youngs for taking in desperate teenaged girls when no one else seemed to care. "They were doing a job that no one else wanted and Lila truly believed in her work... God's work." Yet, even Longley's admiration of Lila was mitigated by his dislike for her as a person. "They were a crummy lot, and I avoided them as much as I possibly could, but I guess I survived longer than any other lawyer." Longley thought others would have found William and Lila insufferable clients because they would never accept legal advice. "I think William would have accepted advice if Lila had not been so forceful."

Denying all knowledge of a baby-peddling scheme, Longley says that couples sometimes made donations of a couple of hundred dollars to the Maternity Home, although these were not mandatory. He has fond memories of the gift-bearing couples. On one occasion, an American couple asked Charles Longley what gift he would like most; on their next visit they brought with them the fishing rod he had requested. Because of the inflated population in Halifax during the war, there was a shortage of basics such as coffee, sugar and butter, as well as luxuries such as silk stockings. Longley laughs when he remembers how women used a popular sandpaper-like depilatory to smooth their legs and then drew a "seam" up the backs with an eyebrow

The Youngs' business flourished in the 1940s, and they were able to expand the Maternity Home.

pencil to make it look as if they were wearing stockings.

Longley's adoption files were destroyed many years ago, so it is impossible to know what the donations to the Home amounted to but, by 1943, the Youngs were well on their way to wealth. Handyman John Rafuse once saw William hand Lila $1,000 for a trip to the United States. John, not sure why Lila was going, assumed that it had something to do with the babies. To John, who was earning $1.50 a day, $1,000 was a "hell of a lot of money" — about three years' wages.

There were outward signs of prosperity as early as February 1939, when the Youngs paid off the mortgage on the Maternity Home, and then built their own home. The three-story clapboard house contained nine bedrooms, three bathrooms, a den, a dining room, a living room and a kitchen. It amply accommodated their five growing children: William, Marshall, Cyril, Isabel and Joy.

Later, the Youngs expanded the dairy farm out back and built a chicken house. Over the next six years they purchased new cars and more than sixty acres of prime real estate in the Chester area, including several ocean-front lots located a short distance from the Maternity Home. Lila and William had five cottages built and painted white, and the shoreline was cleared for a white sand beach. When the tide washed away the sand, men were hired to harrow it back. A pleasure craft was anchored offshore for the Youngs' children and their guests.

Their greatest source of pride was the Maternity Home itself. After additions and expansions, the cottage originally built in 1928 became the centrepiece of a huge structure with fifty-four rooms and fourteen bathrooms. Girls could now reserve private rooms, semiprivate rooms or a bed in the ward. William designed the expansion himself. "My father built that Home," Joy Young recalled, "and it was beautiful, plumb from top to bottom."

Handyman John Refuse helped, boarding in walls, plastering and painting. "The Home was a mansion. It was really something," he said. Elegant turrets rose from the roof of the Home, which was surrounded by expansive lawns and greenery. The Youngs also hired a gardener, and William molded fountains and life-size deer in cement, placing them throughout the gardens, around waterfalls and ponds.

The *piece de résistance* was a handcrafted statue of a gilded infant astride a globe, William's idea. He drew a sketch and one afternoon drove to Robie Coolen's blacksmith shop in Fox Point to have the frame made. Robie fashioned an iron frame of a baby, extending the tailbone to attach to the globe. William built up the frame with mortar, painted the statue gold and mounted it atop one of the Home's pseudo-Norman towers overlooking East Chester. After all the finishing touches had been taken care of, the Youngs had a photograph of thirteen babies and four staff members taken on the lawn in front of the Home.

When completed in 1943, the Maternity Home, mortgage free, was assessed at $40,000. The business, once quiet and unassuming, was large and ostentatious. The Youngs, decked out in expensive furs and finery, were bastions of local society — wealthy, generous, respected, and admired — the baby barons of East Chester.

Chapter 11

Neglect

The illegitimate-baby boom and the developing sales system provided the Youngs with both profits and problems. Business thrived, but the market became demanding. Most couples wanted what they considered to be perfect babies — white with no physical defects. Lawyer Charles Longley remembers couples wanting perfectly formed Caucasians. If infants were black or of mixed race they would be rejected. Moreover, given the maternity and general health standards of the time, many babies were born ill or disabled. By this time, the Youngs' transfer agreement made it clear that certain babies would be rejected:

> It we are unable to find a home for the child we will maintain it for the rest of its natural life for the remarkably small cost of three hundred dollars, provided the child is white, and is not birthmarked, crippled or deformed. Needless to say this is an outstanding offer.

Charles Longley says he was unaware of the practice of feeding certain babies water and molasses until they died, and says he did not notice anything unusual about the health of the babies who were adopted. He had no idea that some babies were allowed to perish through criminal neglect and that others were adopted into less-than-ideal homes. From the case studies available, it is difficult to determine which babies had the kinder fate. The provincial pathologist, Ralph Smith, asked to investigate the death of a boy from the Maternity Home in January 1942, had growing suspicions.

The Halifax *Herald* reported on January 9 that a coroner's jury inquest was investigating the death of a child adopted by Mr. and Mrs. John Wood of Amherst, Nova Scotia. In her testimony, Mrs. Wood said she had paid $25 to transport two infants from the Ideal Maternity Home to her own home in Amherst. One of the babies was ill when he arrived and died soon afterwards. Ralph Smith concluded that the child had suffered from an infection of the middle ear and blood poisoning. Despite his findings, the jury ruled the death was due to natural causes. But before ending the inquiry, the Jury Foreman, Frank J. Elliott, recommended that conditions at the Ideal Maternity Home be investigated.

Follow-up inspections in the Home again failed to uncover serious wrongdoing, but Frank Davis was convinced that William and Lila were not only selling babies but also placing them in unsuitable homes. He had written to Senator William Duff of Lunenburg County a year earlier, in the spring of 1941, telling him the Youngs were "dropping babies out and placing them in slums." William and Lila, friends of Senator Duff, were told about the letter. They were furious and accused Davis of causing them shame and ridicule. The letter may have created temporary embarrassment, but it did little to slow the reckless placement of the less marketable babies who survived the Youngs' purposeful neglect.

There can be little doubt that Sheila Rose Marie LeBlanc, born March 20, 1941, was carelessly placed in a less-than-desirable home. Lila delivered the baby but had no interest in keeping her for adoption because she had developed rickets, a disease in infants caused by a lack of vitamin D, which results in a softening and bowing of the pelvis and legs. At six months, Sheila was thin and pallid, weighing only ten pounds, barely half the normal weight of a baby her age. She was near death when Vivian Brown, an impoverished woman from Lawrencetown, on the eastern shore of Nova Scotia, agreed to take her. Vivian did not have money to pay for a healthy baby, so Lila said, "you can take this sick baby, but she won't live the year ...

she's too weak." Sheila, renamed Betty, survived, but her legs had to be rubbed with oil and exercised in a circular motion for more than a year before they would support her.

Betty Caumartin, born at the Home in March 1941.

In Lawrencetown, Betty lived with her stepmother and two other adopted children in a squalid two-room hovel with a cot, table and chairs. A wooden box for their clothing was kept under the bed where the three children slept. Her stepfather was in the Merchant Navy and away most of the time. Vivian, a tall, thin woman with a shock of red hair, might have had good intentions when she took Betty from the Ideal Maternity Home, but she was incapable of being a caring parent. She drank heavily and entertained sailors. "She would beat us and throw anything close to hand. She said if I ever told Daddy about the men in the house, she would send me back to that awful maternity home."

Betty knew she was adopted and as a child was so lonely she often cried herself to sleep. When she asked Vivian about her birth parents, she was told her mother was French and her father German, but that she did not know their names because the adoption papers were destroyed in a fire. At fourteen, Betty and her family moved to Montreal where she had to leave school and get a job. Her first full-time employment was at Woolworth's Department Store, where she made $20 a week to help support the family. Shy and withdrawn, Betty finally escaped the unhappiness of her home life by getting married at age nineteen.

The marriage failed but Betty was left with three wonderful children. For her, at least, there is a happy ending. Betty eventually remarried; she and her new husband moved with their children to Mascouche, Quebec. "I am prepared to accept what happened to me," she says. "Maybe that's because I am so happy now. I used to hate my stepmother, Vivian, for the way she treated us, but now I wonder if she actually saved my life by getting me out of that Home."

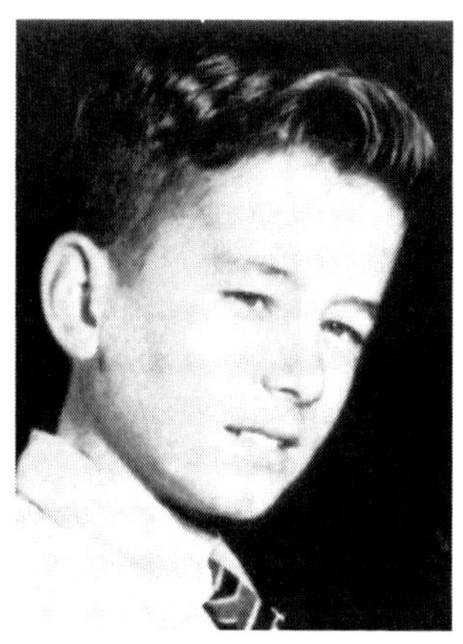

Arthur Wendell White, born at the Home in April 1944.

Arthur Wendell White, born at the Home in April 1944, was another baby Lila Young could not place easily or profitably. Thin, malnourished and suffering from rickets, Wendell was handed over to a couple from Dartmouth. While his adoptive father, an engineer on a Coast Guard ship, was frequently away from home, his adoptive mother, Ginger, entertained other men. Wendell never understood why, as a boy, he had to call so many Blue Bell taxi-drivers uncle.

When he was seven, his "mother," whom he loved dearly, was taken to a hospital for treatment of tuberculosis. Wendell was sent to live with his paternal grandparents in a shabby three-room house with no running water. While there, his grandfather beat him regularly.

In August 1955, at age eleven, Wendell moved into his "father's" small apartment in downtown Halifax, but when his "father" could no longer keep him he was sent to a foster home in Sackville, outside of Halifax, where he was raised by a kind and gentle woman named Edith Legalley. "She was the mother I never had, Wendell says, the only person who ever hugged me and made me feel loved and protected."

During his stay in Sackville, Wendell was fifteen and on his way to milk the cows when received word that his "mother" Ginger had died; the tuberculosis had killed her. It was not until Wendell was a young adult, applying for his birth certificate that he discovered he had been born at the Ideal Maternity Home and that Ginger was not his real mother; the two people he had always thought were his parents were no relation at all. It was then that Wendell began a life long search for his real family.

Chapter 12

Trafficking

LOVELY BABIES FOR ADOPTION
Ideal Maternity Home
East Chester, Nova Scotia

F.R. MacKinnon's suspicions were correct. Even with an operating licence, Lila and William continued breaking the law by placing babies for adoption without approval from the Director of Child Welfare, and they continued advertising their services in the newspaper. The above ad ran in the Halifax *Herald* on December 4, 1942. The ads, along with the Youngs' increasing greed and duplicity, spurred the growth of their business. Inadequate monitoring, ineffective laws and an irresolute cabinet minister allowed it to flourish. In 1943, despite evidence of law-breaking and suspicions of neglect, Frank Davis once again went against F.R. MacKinnon's wishes: he renewed the Youngs' licence. Whether out of cowardice or political expediency, Davis preferred to let the Youngs continue in business rather than deny them a licence.

The increasing supply of wartime babies stimulated both the legitimate adoption business and lucrative baby-selling. Babies from the Ideal Maternity Home were scattered all over the continent to homes both good and wretched. The major market was the northeastern United States; MacKinnon recalls hearing about couples from as far away as South America coming to the Home. He tried to convince Davis to toughen the Maternity Boarding House Act so that the Youngs could be more closely scrutinized, but Davis was reluctant.

"He would pick my brain," MacKinnon said, "trying to

determine if I could support my arguments. He was saying to me, 'If you're so damn smart, then justify your stand.'

"Davis would say, so how do you explain all these people in Lunenburg supporting the Youngs? They think they're providing a useful service. And look at the Halifax Infants' Home, what the girls have to go through there. They're made to feel so guilty. How do you rationalize that?"

MacKinnon argued that the demand for money to deliver babies was unreasonable. The girls were being exploited.

Davis yelled, "Why the hell shouldn't they pay? They got themselves into trouble and their parents can afford to pay."

MacKinnon argued, "They have to pay unreasonable sums, and it's not fair that a couple from New Brunswick, the United States or South America should have to pay $800 or $1,000 for a baby. It's unfair and unreasonable."

"What do you expect me to do? There's only a handful of you on one side saying she is wrong, and there are hundreds, perhaps thousands, supporting the business."

Davis was feeling other pressures, too. In 1943, the public was shocked when Montreal police discovered a number of "baby farms." Unmarried mothers were going to private maternity homes, using false names and leaving their children behind. *The Standard*, a weekly newspaper, reported that once the proper financial arrangement had been made, the babies were "shunted into crèches and baby farms and then sold at so much a head, like puppies." Many were going into orphanages or handed over to individuals without proper supervision. There were no records of the babies, no names, no identification.

Fear of a similar scandal, F.R. MacKinnon's persistence and pressure from the Children's Aid Society eventually encouraged Davis to strengthen Nova Scotia's adoption law. Although he did nothing directly to challenge the Youngs' business practices, he did make it a requirement of the Adoption Act for a child to live with the adoptive parents for one year before adoptions could be finalized. During this year the adopting parents and their home would be assessed. At the year's end the courts would have to be satisfied that the living conditions were suitable for the child.

But William and Lila were clever, and they were getting brilliant legal advice. Sections of the province's Adoption Act excluded businesses that had been incorporated; by incorporating the Ideal Maternity Home, they would not need a licence from the provincial government or consent for adoption, and they could avoid the one-year probation requirement. The Youngs applied for and were granted incorporation status for the Home. No one objected. They proudly publicized their accomplishment in sales pamphlets and spiritual messages sent to friends in the United States.

> Today, with the work fully organized and established as an incorporated adoption agency, [the Home] is now doing a larger and more efficient work for humanity and we pay tribute to HIM who watches even the sparrows when they fall, and we thank HIM also for help and wisdom in its development, and protection when evil influences would injure and hurt its progress.

By this time William and Lila had detected Frank Davis's Achilles' heal — his fear of a public scandal — and they took full advantage. If Davis wanted to gain control over the Ideal Maternity Home, he would have to go through the courts — and suffer the attendant publicity. The Youngs had commercial clout, social support and community support. They established a board of directors: Lila was treasurer and obstetrician; William was vice-president and general manager. Charles Longley was their legal advisor, local businessman George Elliott became their auditor, and Robin S. Hennigar was secretary. Hennigar had been a prominent Chester Basin shipbuilder in the early 1900s, and by the 1940s was a fish-barrel maker and Christmas tree exporter.

But Lila and William knew that to keep Davis and other government officials at bay they had to have a powerful political ally as well. They called upon their friend, the Honourable William Duff. Originally from Newfoundland, Duff was a former mayor of Lunenburg and later a Member of Parliament. He was appointed to the Canadian Senate in February 1936.

Senator William Duff became President of the Ideal Maternity Home's Board of Directors.

Duff, married with three daughters, was said to be a pious man. He was also a millionaire who allegedly leased boats to the rumrunners during prohibition. As president of Chester Basin Shipbuilders Ltd. and the Lunenburg Marine Railway, he had valuable connections in the U.S., which he developed while smuggling liquor from St. Pierre and Miquelon into the western United States. This shadier side of the robust senator was not widely known to people in Lunenburg County, who saw him as a high-ranking Liberal and a father figure in Lunenburg County politics.

At the pinnacle of his career, Duff became President of the Board of Directors of the Ideal Maternity Home. In an impressive brochure advertising the Home, Senator Duff included his own glowing endorsement:

> The birth of an idea came on the first day of February during the winter of 1928 in this humble dwelling in the village of East Chester, Nova Scotia, that was destined to become a mighty factor in the future health and happiness of the rising generation, by the care and development of the babies in Canada. The idea, however, was first conceived in the heart and mind of the founders of the Ideal Maternity Home when they emerged from their Alma Mater qualified for the task they undertook to accomplish. Since the work was different from other endeavors, many difficulties

> were encountered; but with a strong faith in God and determination for the betterment of humanity, obstacles were surmounted, and they nobly pioneered the work of child welfare by developing strong healthy babies with delightful surroundings for both mother and child. The large adoption service conducted by the Ideal Maternity Home has been a help and blessing through the years and has made happy homes all over the Dominion of Canada as well as in distant lands where these charming babies have been adopted.
> William Duff, President

The same brochure featured a large photograph of the son and daughter-in-law of Henry Ernest Kendall, Nova Scotia's Lieutenant Governor from 1942 to 1947. Mr. and Mrs. John Stewart Kendall proudly displayed their new baby, adopted, no doubt without charge, from the Ideal Maternity Home. The Kendalls probably knew nothing about the nefarious side of the adoption business when they provided this testimonial: "To all, into whose hands this book may come, let us say that our home has been made happy by this darling baby girl from the Ideal Maternity Home and we know the joy that can come to those who adopt a child, and we feel that the work being done by the Ideal Maternity Home is worthy of every aid that can be given."

The Youngs also enjoyed the support of many leading citizens of Chester, including the Chester Council. "A lot of those people were merchants who benefited from income at the Home and wanted the Youngs to stay in business," recalled Charles Longley, who addressed the Council several times on the Youngs' behalf. Phil H. Moore, a former president of the Chester Board of Trade, reported in the mid-1940s that the Youngs spent a staggering $50,000 each year in the Chester area. So, like the majority of the Chester Municipal Council, Moore backed them during their lengthy fight with Public Health Minister Frank Davis. East Chester businessmen were

The son and daughter-in-law of Nova Scotia's Lieutenant Governor proudly display the "lovely" baby they adopted from the Ideal Maternity Home.

"extremely solicitous" of the Home and fought every attempt by child-welfare authorities to control the business. The enormous community support and Senator Duff's backing insulated the Youngs from suspicion during their busiest and most profitable years.

While the Youngs were cleverly protecting themselves, two key government officials were taking on added responsibilities. Public Health Minister Davis also became minister of the newly formed Department of Public Welfare in 1943, and F.R. MacKinnon was appointed Director of Child Welfare the following year. Founding members of the Children's Aid Society described MacKinnon as a "vital and dynamic force in the field of social work with a deep consciousness of the needs of the community to promote a better day for the children of adversity."

Soon after his appointment, MacKinnon issued a pamphlet outlining government policies and principles on adoptions. The pamphlet, signed by Frank Davis, stated that the government would "safeguard and uphold the child's interests at all times, and guide and help the mother of the child born out of wedlock, and see to it that she is not imposed upon or exploited, or needlessly deprived of the custody of her child."

Even with MacKinnon's profound commitment to improving conditions for illegitimate children, he could still not obtain evidence of baby selling from the unwed mothers or the adoptive parents. "They were long gone by the time we tried to investigate," he said later. "Even if they were local people, we couldn't walk into their houses and demand to know what they paid for their babies. There were moral limits of decency."

The Youngs' adoption business grew to the point where they hired high-powered lawyers in Saint John and New Jersey to arrange adoptions in the United States. These lawyers developed sophisticated networking to get babies out of Nova Scotia as unobtrusively as possible. On February 25, 1945, Charles Longley wrote to a New Jersey couple to explain the process. To qualify for visas, he said, couples needed a certificate from an employer showing annual income, letters from a bank manager verifying financial status, six photographs of the child they wanted to adopt, a marriage certificate and a receipt for the previous year's income taxes:

> *The first step is to come to East Chester, N.S., and select a baby. When you have taken your child you make application at Saint John, New Brunswick, for a decree of adoption and change of name. This is looked after by our Saint John attorney for a fee of approximately seventy-five dollars.*

Longley's need for personal information to prepare the petition for adoption was understandable but his persistent inquiries about income and assets were more suspect.

> *While the proceedings are being taken, you apply for a Canadian passport for the child. The entire proceeding takes about ten days. Information we must have to prepare petition for adoption: Date of your marriage; your income for the year. Have you any other sources of income other than your salary? Where are you employed? Do you own any bonds? To what value? How much*

do you have in the bank? What insurance do you carry on your lives? Please give name of company and the amount in each case. Do you own your own home? If so, what is its value? Do you own your own furniture? What is the value of it? Do you owe any bills? Give the name of your doctor and clergyman, or any two responsible citizens who would be willing to give an affidavit as to your character. List all assets.

The New Brunswick contact was a highly respected lawyer, Benjamin Rex Guss, who later became a judge in the Family Division of the New Brunswick Provincial Court. Guss was prominent in the Jewish community and had been president of both the Saint John Law Society and the New Brunswick Law Society. He was on the National Council of the Canadian Bar Association and was past president of the Young Conservatives of Canada. In short, he had excellent credentials. Most of the babies Benjamin Guss sent to the U.S. were adopted by Jewish families.

Charles Longley had studied at Dalhousie University Law School with Guss and during those years respected him, but when Guss started working for the Youngs, a fight over how to split the lucrative adoption dollars developed. Longley, threatened by the loss of the business that had served him so well, accused Guss of becoming a "sleazy" lawyer who tried to muscle Longley out of the picture.

"He wanted to take over the whole thing," Longley recalled. "The way he handled it, it was going to be a gold mine for him and the Youngs. The way I handled it, it was just peanuts. He would put the bite on couples to cough up $5,000 or $10,000 if they wanted a child. He wouldn't have called it buying the baby, but what's what it would have amounted to." Longley bitterly recalled that Guss was a great friend of the Chief Justice of the Supreme Court of New Brunswick and that any adoption he was arranging went through quickly and without complication.

Longley was aware of lawyers in the United States who

were in the adoption business to make a fast buck. There were occasions when couples adopting babies trusted lawyers to pass on their donations to the Youngs, but the money was never sent, Longley said. The Youngs' New Jersey attorney was William Kreiger, a bachelor living with two spinster sisters. A typical transaction arranged by Kreiger involved a baby named Louis Lawrence MacKenna. The mother, Anna, became pregnant while her husband was overseas. She gave birth to Louis at the Ideal Maternity Home on January 21, 1945, after which she worked for three months to pay off her bill. Once arrangements had been made to board Louis at the Home, Anna returned to her home in Prince Edward Island.

In April 1946, after her husband came back from the war, Anna went to East Chester to get Louis. Lila told her he had been adopted, and she could not locate the couple who took him. Later, Lila phoned Anna to say she would be able to find the baby but that Anna would have to pay $10,000 to get him back. Anna, astounded, was unable to come up with the money. Her baby was gone. Deeply hurt over the loss, Anna prayed for him every night. She carried a photograph of Louis when he was ten days old throughout her life.

Anna had no way of knowing that when she went to the Home looking for her baby, Louis was still there, but Lila was saving him for an American couple who had made arrangements to adopt him. In July, three months after Anna had left East Chester, William Kreiger sent an older Jewish couple from South Orange, New Jersey, to the Ideal Maternity Home. The Reiders were well off. Albert owned a clothing manufacturing company in Manhattan and Florence was an office manager for a large corporation. Their home was elegant, complete with maids, a nanny and a cook.

When Albert and Florence Reider arrived at the Maternity Home they saw a "pretty, well-dressed baby girl" sitting with her mother on the steps of the Home. Soon after, Florence was saddened when she realized the mother must have been waiting for her baby's new family. The Reiders did not immediately choose Louis MacKenna; they had hoped to take home a girl. However, the girl they selected could not be released because the natural mother had insisted she be placed with a Catholic family. Albert Reider then chose Sammy, a boy with black hair and dark eyes, whom the Youngs said had a Jewish father. The Reiders did not believe the story, but decided to take him anyway. When it was discovered that Sammy was deaf in one ear, they decided to choose another baby, as it might be difficult to arrange for a child with a disability to gain legal status in the United States.

As Florence Reider moved through the nursery, she noticed many three- and four-year-olds running around. "They looked like wild animals," she said later. "None of the children had enough clothes on, and there didn't seem to be anyone supervising them." When sixteen-month-old Louis reached out from his crib and grabbed her coat, she picked him up. Louis, with blonde hair and blue eyes, was malnourished and unusually small and immobile for his age, but this was the baby she wanted. Through the New Jersey lawyer the Reiders paid a $300 donation to the Maternity Home and fees of nearly $10,000 to their lawyer. Louis MacKenna became Michael Reider.

Lila told the Reiders there would be a one-week delay before the deal could be finalized. Albert Reider took a steamer back to New Jersey; Florence stayed behind and shopped for antique silver. With the paperwork completed, Florence returned home to New Jersey with her new baby. Soon afterwards, William Kreiger demanded an intermediary's fee of $3,000. The Reiders refused, but Kreiger harassed them for several months before giving up.

When Michael grew older, he learned about his parents' visit to East Chester. Under New Jersey law, they did not qualify as adoptive parents because of their age and medical history. Florence Reider was forty-three. Albert was nearly sixty and undergoing electric-shock therapy. (It was later discovered that he suffered from Addison's disease, characterized by progressive anemia, debility and brown discolouration of the skin.) Nonetheless, the Reiders were able to take Michael from Canada into New Jersey and have the adoption legalized there. It was not until Michael was an adult inquiring about his Canadian roots that he suspected his removal from Canada and his adoption had not been officially sanctioned by the Nova Scotia government. Michael was curious about the legality of his adoption, and he wanted to know if his birth mother had willingly signed documents giving him up. Michael Reider would return to Canada one day and find the answers he was searching for.

For increasing numbers of people involved in the adoption of infants, money was no object. Desperate young women and their often more desperate parents wanted their problems solved with minimal fuss. Childless couples hungered for the fulfillment of parenthood. The demand for babies generated more money than William and Lila ever imagined. They also realized the lawyers handling the adoptions were drawing greater profits than they were so they fired Benjamin Guss. In September 1945, William wrote to friends in the U.S.

> *I am glad to be able to tell you that we are now able to put through adoptions right here in Nova Scotia at once, at way less cost, if the adopting parents can bring with them a certificate from the State Welfare Department setting forth the approval of their home as a suitable place in which to bring up a child. If they can bring this valuable document with them, it is a simple matter and the cost is negligible and will save a great deal of time and cost, and travel as well. I hope as many as possible who come, will be interested in adopting boys. On the other hand we have a splendid variety of younger girls but not so many older ones. But in any case we will see that they get just the baby they want, and they will have ninety to choose from. Quite a few are coming from the United States and more than usual from Nova Scotia.*

To describe William and Lila's adoption business as a gold mine may seem callous, as the Home provided a sorely needed public service. Moreover, calculation of revenues for the Ideal Maternity Home involves conjecture and guesswork. Lila Young reported in 1936 that babies were born during the two previous years at a rate of one every nine days, roughly 40 a year. Nova Scotia government records show that 209 mothers registered at the Home between 1941 and 1943, an average of about 70 a year. Correspondence between the Home and a former resident in 1946 was stamped with the number 803, indicating the official number of babies born since the Youngs were first obliged to keep a register in 1940. Charles Longley reported that he handled 15 to 20 adoptions every month between 1941 and 1946. Records of government inspections of the Home throughout the 1940s reported between 70 and 125 babies at a time there. This suggests a minimum of 1,500 babies were born at the Home from 1937 to 1947.

In the mid-1940s, pregnant girls were paying an average of $400 for services at the Home, generating annual revenues of about $60,000 for the Youngs. But the real money was in baby sales. Babies were sold for between $1,000 ad $10,000 each. On top of that, donations were demanded. Even allowing for the "rejected" babies and those who died — at least ten percent of the total — and sales to the less lucrative local market, it is reasonable to estimate that half the babies, 700 or so, were sold for an average of about $5,000. That is a total of $3.5 million. However conservative the calculation, the Ideal Maternity Home was big business. No wonder the Youngs fiercely resisted all interference.

Lila, more than William, resented any interference. Egocentric and arrogant, she became fixated on success, using religious self-righteousness to defend her actions. Any good intentions she might have had in the beginning had dissipated. The social values of the day, the condemnation of women who became pregnant out of wedlock, the lax regulations and the religious tone of the Home all helped Lila in the deception that became the Ideal Maternity Home.

Chapter 13

God on Their Side

Lila and William Young's unorthodox business practices frustrated Frank Davis, but to him their most offensive trait was their willingness to ignore religious policies on adoption and foster care. Davis, not a particularly religions man, resented the Youngs' cavalier disregard of tradition that no one else dared to challenge publicly, even if the circumstances warranted.

In the mid-1940s, Children's Aid Societies in Nova Scotia were having difficulty placing children; they had a surplus of Catholic babies needing homes, but a shortage of Catholic couples wanting to adopt or become foster parents. The surplus of babies was likely a direct result of the government's refusal to allow Catholic babies to go into non-Catholic homes.

Ironically, Davis's stand on religion was offensive to at least one top official in his own department: F.R. MacKinnon found the religious policy difficult to defend because it meant Jewish couples were restricted from adopting. The policy "irked a lot of Jewish people," he said later. "They felt such a policy unnecessary and unreasonable." There was a large Jewish community wanting to adopt and the official process was closed to them. F.R. MacKinnon had Jewish friends who desperately wanted to adopt children. "To be honest, I told them how to break the law. I advised them to go to Quebec to adopt children because in that province the government didn't have a religious policy. And when they returned to Nova Scotia I assured them that the government here wouldn't intervene."

Charles Longley did not hesitate to help the Youngs place babies in Jewish homes. Like Lila, he believed newborn infants did not have a religion. "The religion of a baby is acquired from whomever raises him," he says. "Lila used to say that a baby had no religion and that it would go to heaven whether it was baptized or not." Longley recalls that the U.S. Consul-General's office had, by then, waived the religious policies in that country. Consul officials were more concerned with couples having proper documentation showing they would be acceptable parents. "They were meticulous in their investigations of couples, checking them out morally and financially," Longley says. "The Consul-General's office would not have issued visas to these people if they were unable to cope with a child. The very fact that they wanted babies was in their favour, but the welfare department here treated these people terribly."

Longley frequently had confrontations with Frank Davis over the policy. He wanted the minister to add a clause to the Adoption Act specifically stating that religion was not a factor. At one point, Davis told him bluntly, "If you want a new adoption law you should draft one yourself." Longley took the suggestion seriously and spent considerable time drafting a law that did not adhere to religion. Prior to submitting his draft proposal, he took it to the American Consul-General, who told Longley it was a wonderful submission and encouraged Longley to present it to the Nova Scotia government. That was the only praise Longley ever received.

When he approached Frank Davis, the intransigent health minister tossed the proposal aside, saying that it certainly was not the kind of law he wanted. Clearly, Davis was not about to back down on the religious restriction. "Davis was an outright bigot," Longley said later. "He was intolerant, a puritanical person of the worst kind." On the other hand, Longley thought F.R. MacKinnon one of the few in government with good instincts. He had compassion for the mothers and for the couples wanting to adopt. "His problem was that he was under Davis's thumb," Longley said.

When William and Lila began selling babies on a large scale, the narrow restrictions of Nova Scotia's religious community worked in their favour in two ways. First, they were able to exploit a mother's desire for a specific religion for her baby. The transfer agreement of the mid-1940s between the Home and the mother stated that girls had to pay $50 over and above the $300 basic charge if they wanted their babies to go to couples of a particular faith. Second, the Youngs' willingness to sell across religious lines brought premium prices. Wealthier couples came immediately when they learned there was an agency in Nova Scotia not adhering to religion in the adoption process.

Many stayed at the Casa Blanca Guest Home, one of Chester's finest inns, which opened at the end of the Second World War. Its owner, Isabel Marshall, a diminutive woman with a round face and small pale blue eyes, sought to make their three- to five-day visits as comfortable as possible. She accompanied them to the Maternity Home to visit the babies and celebrated when they became proud parents. She even packed special formula for each baby's trip home.

The couples who stayed with Isabel were usually unable to have children of their own and could not find any to adopt. "They told me Jewish children were very seldom put up for adoption. They had their names in Jewish adoption agencies for years and never received a word from any of them. These people told me that Jewish illegitimate children were almost nonexistent because Jewish families, proud and self-reliant, looked after their own."

The couples' stay at the Casa Blanca was busy; they met lawyers, visited their babies, and waited for the paperwork to be completed. Couples usually insisted the birth mother sign a document releasing the child to them. Some also arranged for medical check-ups by Dr. Barrie Coward, the only pediatrician Lila Young recommended.

Isabel remembers that the couples were usually wealthy, with "jewels, expensive wrist watches and fine clothing." The worn red-and-black guest book, the Casa Blanca's register from 1945, is filled with signatures of couples from New York, Pennsylvania, and New Jersey. "The guests who came here talked a great deal about Hitler's Holocaust," Isabel recalls. "So many of their friends and relatives who became prisoners in the German concentration camps had been piled up like cordwood and burned. Sometimes complete families were wiped out. For the people who came here, having a child who could carry on the family name was very, very important," Isabel remembers. "It was an exciting time ... you couldn't help but feel happy for these people. They would come into the kitchen and throw their arms around my neck and cry. It meant so much to have a child. It's odd, though," Isabel mused, "it's odd to think that in little Nova Scotia we would be affected by the likes of Hitler, but we were."

If religious narrowness plagued the mothers of illegitimate babies, it sometimes also followed the babies into their new adoptive worlds. Even being born a healthy white baby at the Ideal Maternity Home was no guarantee of a life of religious tolerance. Sandy Tuckerman, born on June 1, 1945, was one of the more sought after babies. Named June Ellen at birth, she was healthy, without any visible birthmarks or defects. She was adopted by a Newark, New Jersey, couple in their mid-forties who were unable to have their own children. After visiting the Ideal Maternity Home and seeing June, with her dark hair and brown eyes, they decided the asking price — $1,000 — was within their means.

While waiting for the adoption arrangements to be completed, the couple spent a few hours each day at the Home caring for June. During this time, they grew fond of a blonde three-year-old boy, who was desperate for attention. Lila, eager to strike a profitable deal, suggested they take the boy as well. But the dark-haired couple were members of a strict Orthodox synagogue, and they thought a blonde, fair-skinned boy would always seem an outsider in their world. With regret, they left him behind.

Baby June, meanwhile, became ill; she was feverish and vomiting. When she could not longer retain baby formula, her new parents wrapped her in warm blankets and drove her to a doctor in Halifax, where she was diagnosed with pneumonia. She eventually recovered and was flown to her new home in New Jersey, where she was renamed Sandy and raised in strict Jewish tradition. As a child, Sandy had a favourite bedtime story about where she came from and how she was chosen. "My mother used to tell me that when she flew to Nova Scotia to visit the Home, there were eighty-five babies to choose from, but she picked me because I was fat and beautiful. She told me this story over and over again and I never tired of it."

As Sandy grew older, her mother tried to discourage her curiosity about her origins. She would only say that Sandy's birth mother died during childbirth and that her father died in the war, a story Sandy never believed. Her adoptive father seemed better equipped to handle his daughter's inquisitive nature, explaining that they had to pay money to the Youngs. "My mother used to interrupt and say they didn't have to pay for me, they simply made a donation so the rest of the babies left behind could be cared for."

Sandy's parents became friends with other couples, almost all Jewish, who had also adopted babies from the Home. The cost, $1,000 to $10,000, was a fortune to most of them. (Based on the consumer price index, $10,000 in 1940 would be the equivalent of more than $103,000 in 2006.) A doctor and his wife, friends of Sandy's adoptive parents, paid the Youngs $3,000 for two boys. Sandy also remembers a visitor arriving at their door when she was a girl; he asked for a donation to the Home. He said it would have to close if the Youngs did not receive financial help. "My parents gave additional money, as did the other parents."

Sandy loved her parents, but like many adopted children she felt she did not belong. She knew she was adopted, but still found herself looking through the family photograph albums searching for a resemblance that was not there. Her curiosity and feelings of isolation intensified as she grew older. Her mother, frequently ill from a nervous disorder, was very protective. "She used to screen the television shows I watched and decided which friends I should play with. When I was seven or eight, I was sent to summer camp where all the children were Jewish. For a long time I didn't realize there was anyone in the world who was not Jewish."

Sandy Tuckerman, adopted by a Jewish couple in New Jersey, felt she never belonged.

During the school year, Sandy would study Hebrew in the mornings, English in the afternoons and, after regular school hours, would attend Hebrew classes at another school. June was forbidden to mention her adoption to anyone outside the family. "It was almost as if she was afraid she would lose me if anyone found out, so it had to be secretive."

As a child, Sandy believed she had been born Jewish, but at age eight she realized she was different when her parents insisted that she participate in a religious ceremony. "It was similar to a baptism, but more like a process of new beginning. We went into this brick building; the room was dark and gloomy and it smelled musty." Sandy became upset when she had to remove all her clothing to allow the women to wash her hair and body with soap and water. She had to be cleansed of her sins, they said. She became terrified by being completely immersed in a mikveh, a pool of natural water, while a rabbi said prayers. "It was a horrible, horrible experience," Sandy says. "I had no idea what prayers they were saying. I was terrified. I used to run away, but they brought me back. It was that important to my mother."

When she was twelve, she encountered another emotional

setback. Days before she was to have her *bat mitzvah* — a ceremony celebrating the age of maturity for girls — the rabbi came to her home to say she could not participate because she was a converted Jew. "That created a terrible mess," Sandy recalls. Her parents had to find another rabbi who agreed to put her through the special ceremony. "It always seemed as though my mother was trying so hard to make me Jewish, and even as a small child, I knew there was something wrong. I used to ask her why I had to do this and where did I really come from. I would say 'Mommy, what was I before?'" Sandy's mother adamantly refused to discuss it.

The most upsetting incident occurred when Sandy was preparing to marry Arthur, who was Jewish, but not particularly religious. The Orthodox rabbi who was to perform the ceremony contacted Sandy the night before the wedding to say he had to cancel. He had discovered Sandy was not Jewish by birth and her husband-to-be was not Orthodox. "I was so upset, I cried and cried. I thought we would have to cancel everything." Arthur, furious, insisted the marriage would take place the following day even if they had to find a justice of the peace. Fortunately, Sandy's aunt located another rabbi who agreed to perform the ceremony.

After the wedding, she lost interest in all religion. "I just didn't feel as if I belonged, and if they couldn't accept me … and my husband, then I didn't want anything to do with them." As a young woman, free to make her own decisions, Sandy today describes herself as having no religion. Even the dark hair that had facilitated her adoption into a Jewish family is gone. She dyed it red.

PART III

Gathering Storm 1945–1947

are under the supervision of a Baby Specialist who sees that a solid foundation is laid in each case for the development of a strong mind and body, and only clean, healthy babies are placed for adoption.

BABY LAND

Chapter 14

Dirty Politics

In the fall of 1945, with a provincial election looming, Lila, flamboyant as ever, publicly boasted about the Home's many successful adoptions into the United States. She spent copious amounts of money holding political rallies throughout Lunenburg County, where she campaigned vigorously against the incumbent MLA, Frank Roy Davis. Davis realized this was much more than a case of slander that could be handled in the courts. It was a very personal feud that had exploded into a public confrontation and serious political threat.

His retaliation resulted in intensified inspections at the Maternity Home. During the summer and fall of 1945, he had F.R. MacKinnon visit the Home at least three times. What he found was far worse than he had seen at earlier inspections. During one visit on a hot summer afternoon in early August, as MacKinnon and the Superintendent of Nurses, Margaret MacKenzie, pulled into the driveway, they noticed that all the windows in the building were shut. Inside they found the air stale and foul smelling. Not only was the ventilation inadequate, but none of the babies or small children had been taken out to enjoy the fresh air, even though it was a bright sunny day.

As they moved through the nurseries, the inspectors noticed "flies in abundance," drawn, they assumed, to the open milk containers in the nurseries. It was not long before they could see why the babies were not outside. MacKinnon counted eighty babies and only one girl on duty. They found eight or nine babies crammed into a small dirty room. And the infants were not clearly identified. Nametags were carelessly stuck to walls or on cribs; it would have been easy to mix them up.

When they checked the infants more closely, Margaret MacKenzie became alarmed. They were dirty, as though they had not been bathed for some time. Some were "lying in vomit," while others were in "soiled linen." Their bodies were red and sore from "scalding urine." As there were no isolation quarters, the sick babies were kept in the same room as the healthy ones. After interviewing the girl on duty, MacKenzie concluded that doctors or nurses were never called to the Home, and no one was overseeing nutrition. One of the infants MacKinnon and MacKenzie would have seen that day was Donna Marie Austin, who looked much younger than her six months because she was so thin. Healthy babies her age usually weighed between twenty and twenty-five pounds; Donna Marie weighed only eleven pounds.

Lila was not present during the August inspection, and afterward she was angry to learn the inspectors were permitted to move freely through the institution in her absence. After that inspection, Lila issued strict instructions that no one be allowed inside without her approval. Lila also stepped up her political campaign against Frank Davis, who, she rightly thought, was behind the "harassment." She held rallies at local community halls that often attracted several hundred people. She criticized the laws requiring probationary periods before adoptions could be finalized. Lila's attacks were beyond political; they were downright vicious. "The war is over," she shouted, "but another Hitler has come to Nova Scotia. Do away with Davis and dictatorship."

Child Welfare officials throughout the province jumped to Davis's defence. Glynnford P. Allen, President of the Nova Scotia Association of Children's Aid Societies, paid special tribute to Davis at a Kiwanis Club luncheon. Allen did not mention the Ideal Maternity Home by name, but condemned the practice of sending adoption price lists and maternity home brochures through the mail. He warned against the dangers arising from "hasty placements" of a "mail-order adoption plan." The purpose of the probationary period, Allen said, was to determine whether the child was developing normally and was suitable to the home. The government's licensing requirement prevents "undesirable people from exploiting illegitimate children — alias a black market."

As the hostility heightened, Lila resorted to one of her more lethal weapons: private and confidential information from Maternity Home files. She let it be known that the son of the Deputy Public Health Minister had fathered an illegitimate child born at the Home. She was careful not to make the accusation "on the record" in public, but made certain the story was sufficiently circulated to reach officials in the Public Health and Public Welfare Departments. The story was never verified as true or false; still, it was disconcerting for those in the department. MacKinnon later noted that such blackmail tactics would not have softened Davis's approach towards the Youngs. "Davis was a wily politician who knew his politics, but I don't think he would permit the likes of that to influence him."

But Lila's campaigning techniques had their effect on her family, the Coolens of Fox Point. Even Frederick, the magistrate, who had always supported Lila, was embarrassed by her behaviour. Lila had always been fond of Frederick — the brother who helped raise bail money when she was charged in connection with Eva Nieforth's death, the justice of the peace who sympathized with her when putative fathers refused to pay their bills, her defender when she felt she was under attack by the politicians. Now Frederick withdrew his support.

It soon became evident that Lila was capable of turning on anyone who did not take her side. She publicly disowned Frederick. She had his obituary published in the local newspaper because as far as Lila was concerned, Frederick was dead to her. Weeks later, Frederick received a blistering letter headed "Without Prejudice" and signed by William P. Young. The letter accused Frederick of being, among other things, a traitor no better that Davis and MacKinnon and Lila's other enemies. Frederick suspected Lila had dictated the letter. After reading it, he took a pencil, wrote "My Friends" on the envelope, and stored it in his big roll-top desk, where it remained until after his death in 1962.

While Lila continued her attacks on government, William tried to hold the adoption business together. On September 18, 1945, he wrote to American couples wanting babies and encouraged them to come soon. He also updated them on the election campaign: "We appreciate your kind interest, and I might add that our campaign against Dr. Davis is going over in a big way. In the six lectures already held, we have spoken to about three thousand people. It is costing us considerably, but we feel that any sacrifice is necessary for these helpless babies."

With the election only three weeks away, Frank Davis decided F.R. MacKinnon should make another surprise visit to the Maternity Home. This time he would go armed with a team of medical experts: Lunenburg's Divisional Medical Health Officer, Dr. J.S. Robinson; Halifax pediatrician, Dr. Barrie Coward; and the Superintendent of Nurses, Margaret MacKenzie. During their half-hour wait for Lila's arrival, they heard a great deal of commotion in the nurseries. Later, during one of the court cases involving the Youngs, it was revealed that during inspections girls staying at the Home had been posing as nurses.

Eventually Lila stormed in with lawyer R. Clifford Levy of Chester in tow. During the election campaign, Lila and William hired Levy to represent them. Lunenburg County was a riding with dual representation, and Levy was one of two Progressive Conservative candidates challenging Frank Davis.

With Lila and her lawyer present, F.R. MacKinnon and his colleagues began their inspection. There were eighty babies still in the nurseries, but Donna Marie Austin was not among them. Weeks before this inspection, she was fortunate enough to have been adopted by a couple who put her on a special diet to restore her vitality. During the inspection, MacKinnon found that conditions had generally improved. "The nurseries and the cots were cleaner. The flies weren't so thick." Six of the 80 babies were outside playing.

But Dr. Barrie Coward was highly critical of the Home. Serious overcrowding, inadequate staffing, non-existent medical care and poor diets were all serious problems. Dr. Coward reported that the Home still did not isolate children with infectious diseases such as conjunctivitis and colds, and the babies were still not getting enough fresh air and exercise. He was told the children over eighteen months were taken outdoors every day and the babies nine to eighteen months were taken out when possible. The youngest infants were kept indoors.

Not surprisingly, Dr. Coward's main concern was malnutrition. The youngest babies appeared fairly healthy, he said, but the older babies were pale and thin, their tissues soft and their bellies distended. Dr. Coward later explained: "An infant three months old can live on milk alone; that would be a normal diet as long as he gets enough to meet his needs. But to have a nineteen-month-old child living on milk alone would result in serious nutritional problems, and the child would not develop properly. Those children would be prone to infection." But at no point was Dr. Coward or anyone else prepared to suggest any of the infants were starving. Lila was again refusing to comply with the law that required the submission of birth and death records, so Davis was unable to assess the mortality rate, but he suspected it was high.

The increased surveillance at the Home drove Lila and William to become more politically aggressive. In the weeks before the election, they paraded through the streets of Lunenburg County with speakers mounted on top of their car blaring, "End dictatorship — Defeat Davis." Lila shouted while William drove. Ray Corkum and others in the neighbourhood still remember the spectacle.

On a Monday night, a week before the election, Davis tried to remain calm and courteous before a crowded Liberal rally in Lunenburg County's Parish Hall. He announced that the Youngs' slander campaign against him had been contrived by the Progressive Conservative Party. The fifty-seven-year-old Davis, white haired and red faced, suggested the voters seated before him were "too intelligent to fall for a campaign of slander."

He responded to the accusations of Hitlerism by suggesting "a Mrs. Goebbels has come to Nova Scotia who evidently believes that if the truth is misrepresented often enough it will eventually be believed." He challenged the Conservative candidate to "get away from women's petticoats and tell the public where he stands in relation to this scandal." Davis felt compelled to counter the accusations against him and defend the Adoption Act and Maternity Boarding House Act — laws that he said all maternity homes except one complied with. The Adoption Act, requiring a one-year probationary period, was opposed by the Youngs, he said, because they "stood to lose financially" if they obeyed it. The large crowd was attentive as Davis read letters from various service organizations, including the Children's Aid Society and the Red Cross, all supporting the probationary period.

Four days before the election, Davis gave notice that he was suing the *Bridgewater Bulletin and South Shore Record* for "false and malicious libel." Several days earlier, Lila had argued that the *Bridgewater Bulletin and South Shore Record* should print her description of "the real" Frank Davis. She paid the newspaper to print posters, which she distributed throughout the community:

RESTORE DEMOCRACY!

By making October 23rd V-D victory over Davis and Dictatorship. The voters of this fair county face a solemn responsibility on October the 23rd since a war has just been fought to end dictatorship in Europe. We can't afford to let it continure here, so away with Davis and Dictatorship! And since Dr. Davis boasted at the Liberal Convention that Mr. Romkey has been

> in complete accord with everything he has done, we must do away with him also politically, so that people may live without being in fear.

An embarrassed newspaper editor, F.J. Macpherson, reacted swiftly by issuing a front-page apology to Davis, explaining he was out of town when the Youngs asked that the accusations be published in the paper and printed on posters. Macpherson said the newspaper employee who handled the request decided not to print the statement in the *Bridgewater Bulletin* on the grounds that it made "charges against specified individuals." However, thinking he was obligated to accept printing work, he produced the posters and delivered them to the Youngs. By the time Macpherson had returned to the newspaper office, it was too late to recall the posters. The apology continued:

> Unfortunately, these posters made accusations against Dr. Davis which I do not believe to be true, and if I had been in my office from the time they were ordered until the time they were delivered I would have seen they were destroyed. I am writing this article of my own free will and giving it front page publicity simply for the purpose of dissociating myself from the contents of the said posters and in an attempt to make an honourable amend to Dr. Davis for the mistake of one of my employees.

Three days before the election, Davis delivered a writ to Lila Young. In the statement of claim filed in the Supreme Court, Davis stated that the libel had caused great injury to his character and reputation and that he had been "subjected to contempt, hatred, scorn, and ridicule." Davis's lawyer said that to suggest his client was guilty of the bizarre incidents printed in the handbills was the equivalent of saying he was guilty of indictable offences. Davis sought damages and an injunction restraining the Youngs from publishing any further accusations.

The trial would not take place until after the election.

On election night, Lila could barely contain her rage. Her nemesis, Frank Roy Davis and the Liberals swept the province, winning twenty-eight of thirty seats. In Lunenburg County, Davis defeated R. Clifford Levy by more than one thousand votes, but it was clear Lila's campaign had caused some damage. Davis's support in East Chester, where the Youngs campaigned against him, had dropped significantly.

For Lila there was no turning back. She had become greedy, power hungry and ruthless, seeking survival at all cost. So blinded was Lila by her hatred for Davis, that she was unable to see the beginning of the end. The Youngs had enjoyed seventeen profitable years in the adoption business, but the government was finally catching up with them. The Maternity Boarding House Act of 1940 was amended to include incorporated companies. William and Lila applied for an operating licence and were turned down. On November 17, 1945, based on findings from his inspections, F.R. MacKinnon was finally able to order the Ideal Maternity Home closed.

He wrote to the Youngs and explained that a licence could not be issued unless the Director of Child Welfare was satisfied that the operator of the Home was "fit" and the Home itself suitable. MacKinnon offered the Youngs a chance to qualify for a licence if they made dramatic improvements at the Maternity Home. He made twenty-three recommendations, seven of which Lila and William rejected outright:

1) The fixed fee schedule had to be abolished.
2) Adequate records, containing the name, age, weight and diet for each child, had to be kept in the nurseries.
3) Children over six had to be immunized against diphtheria, whooping cough and scarlet fever, and children over one had to be vaccinated against smallpox.
5) Diets must be supervised by a pediatrician.
6) Children being adopted had to be examined by a doctor.
7) Care of babies to be supervised daily by a doctor or nurse.

On refusing the licence, MacKinnon returned the Youngs' application fee — a cheque for $2.15. Shortly thereafter he was quoted as saying, "The peddling of illegitimate babies in Nova Scotia is through."

MacKinnon and Davis were naive to expect their long fight with the Youngs would end so easily. It was just a matter of time before they would resurface. The political campaign had cost the Youngs dearly, and Davis's libel suit loomed as a serious financial threat. William started drinking heavily and disappearing for long periods. Charles Longley, still representing the Youngs from time to time, recalls seeing William "wimping around and doing a little chiropractic work on the side." He suspected William was "messing around" with some of the girls. "My suspicion was that William was a sexy fellow, in a way, and Lila wasn't... well, I think he was interested in playing around with these girls. Knowing they had already slipped once... maybe they would slip again, and Lila being such a bull-headed tartar was not very attractive."

As William became less reliable, it was left to Lila to determine how to proceed with the libel case. She asked Charles Longley to submit a written defence stating that the accusations against Davis during the election campaign were true and could be proven.

1) Lila charged that in November 1933, Davis issued instructions to Queenie Nauss of the registry of Births and Deaths in Chester to withhold burial permits for all deaths at the Maternity Home, and these instructions resulted in a stillborn child being kept unburied on the premises for three weeks. This delay in burial jeopardized the health of the Maternity Home owners and the female residents.
2) In March 1935, the body of a woman from Chester Basin [Constance Hatt's autopsy] was removed from her casket and "placed on a barn door while her internal organs were removed. Then she was sewed up with ordinary twine with the old-fashioned grandmother's stitch. She was then thrust

back into her casket in a disorderly manner for burial."

3) In May 1936 [Eva Nieforth trial], Frank Davis had the Youngs locked up in a county jail in Bridgewater and he forced them to stand trial for alleged crimes of which they were innocent.

The Youngs complained about the 1937–38 order that resulted in RCMP investigations into every death at the Home. They accused Frank Davis of arbitrarily refusing them a licence in 1945, which they claimed, resulted in serious financial loss and public contempt. They said they were "constantly harassed without valid reason or lawful excuse." Finally they accused Davis of obstructing their efforts to find desirable homes for the babies.

When Longley gave a copy of his submission to Lila, she was ecstatic. "She read it and said it was the most wonderful thing," Longley recalls. "That was the defence they were looking for." Lila especially liked the part where Longley described how a woman was laid out on a barn door for an autopsy. After reading it, Lila shouted enthusiastically, "Willie, give this fellow an extra $20 for this wonderful defence!" Longley, believing he had done what any defence lawyer would do, felt insulted by the gesture.

The Statement of Defence was delivered to Public Health Minister Davis in December 1945; seven months later, Charles Longley received notice that "the plaintiff hereby wholly discontinues this action." Davis had dropped the libel suit without explanation. Charles Longley thought he knew why. "We defended it and he dropped it like a hot potato because he couldn't face that tartar... in court she would have torn him to pieces. She would have been vicious and critical of the Health Department. Davis would have been too thin-skinned to have tolerated that."

There probably is a lot of truth in Charles Longley's assessment. Davis had always feared public criticism and would have been reluctant to flirt with yet another scandal. Besides, he had won the election with his reputation intact, and his old friend Premier Angus L. Macdonald was giving him new responsibilities. Along with the Public Health and Public Welfare portfolios, he was about to become minister of Municipal Affairs. Moreover, by denying them an operating licence, Davis knew he now could take on the Youngs in a more impersonal, bureaucratic way. If they continued in the adoption business, he would have the police pursue them through the courts.

Chapter 15

Crack-Down in Two Countries

When the people of Lunenburg County read their newspapers in the fall of 1945 they saw full-page stories on the desperate food shortages in liberated Europe, advertisements reminded people that meat rationing was in effect in Nova Scotia, and the local exhibition was charging twenty-five cents for a viewing of a captured German submarine. In the small print of the classified section, Lila and William Young were still boldly advertising "Lovely Babies For Adoption."

What they would not have read was that Frank Davis had begun a systematic counter-attack against the Youngs and their Ideal Maternity Home. With the help of the RCMP and Immigration officials, he tracked down couples in the United States who had adopted babies from the East Chester home. Davis located five infants who had been taken out of the country between November 1945 and March 1946 without government approval.

Charles Longley, who helped arrange some of the adoptions, was infuriated over the government intervention, particularly the RCMP's decision to go to the homes of American couples who had adopted babies and registered the adoptions in their states. "They questioned them and advised them that the adoptions were against the law," Longley said. "I didn't think they had any business molesting these people that way. They tried to put pressure on them, but these people were very determined. They had already been through quite a bit to get to the stage where they had a baby, and they weren't going to give up easily. It was a scare tactic, really."

The RCMP reported that Katherine Elaine Kennedy was

adopted by the Schmidts of Pittsburgh; Doreen Dawn Grover was adopted by the Rosenthals of Pittsburgh; Donald Arthur Buckler was adopted by the Goldsteins of New York; David Hartling went to the Levinsons of New York; and Roderick Joseph Brown was adopted by the Greenbergs of Brooklyn, New York.

The last baby, Roderick Brown, was born two days before Christmas 1945. His mother, Rose Agnes Brown, a thirty-three-year-old hairdresser in Sydney, Cape Breton, was married with three children. This fourth pregnancy was an accident; she did not want the baby.

Rose's mother-in-law had arranged for her to travel to the East Chester maternity home and agreed to pay the $458 fee. When Rose arrived, she signed the usual contracts giving William power of attorney. After giving birth and returning to Sydney, she received a letter from the Maternity Home, signed by William's personal secretary:

> *Following your recently sent form of affidavit of consent; would you kindly have this paper [release form] sworn and returned to this office as quickly as possible as your baby has been chosen by a grand U.S. couple, where he will receive all life has to offer any child. I feel that should you know this couple personally that you would be as pleased over the placement as we are. Thank you for your early consideration.*
> *Faithfully Yours,*
> *Mrs. Jean Feader for*
> *Dr. Wm P. Young*

The Youngs had investigated the couple from New York and found they had the financial means to qualify as adoptive parents. Bertha and Jack Greenberg, both in their early thirties, lived in a four-room apartment that had electricity and steam heating. He worked as a cutter in the men's clothing industry and had a yearly income of $3,500. The Greenbergs also had bonds and other assets totaling $14,500. Their rabbi wrote to the Youngs on March 4, 1946.

> *I the undersigned, and the Rabbi of the Machizke Talmud Torah of 1315-43 St., Brooklyn, New York. I have known Mrs. Bertha and Jack Greenberg for the past eighteen years. They are members of my congregation and also live in the same neighborhood. They are fine upright people and I think they have much to offer this baby which they would like to adopt. In my estimation they are capable of giving it a fine home and everything else that is necessary.*
> *Yours very truly,*
> *Rabbi S.M. Shapiro*

Their doctor, Irwin J. Kernis, wrote: "This is to certify that I have known Mr. and Mrs. Jack Greenberg for the past eight years. To the best of my knowledge they have always been normal healthy people."

Baby Roderick was sent to the Greenbergs' home, even though the adoption had not been approved by the Nova Scotia government. Frank Davis's officials were able to trace the adoption, in part because New Jersey authorities were also cracking down on illegal adoptions. They helped Davis locate fourteen couples who had adopted from a "Canadian baby market."

In the fall of 1945, a Trenton, New Jersey, newspaper reported that the smuggling scheme had been uncovered by Dr. Ellen C. Potter, Director of Medicine in the Department of Institutions and Agencies in the U.S. She reported that this "boom in Canadian adoptions" occurred because of an advertisement in the local press. The advertisement was promptly removed when the editor learned that a fifty-year-old law forbade it. "Federal naturalization laws are involved when parents adopt children from outside the country," Potter said. "The children do not become U.S. citizens unless they are readopted in this country."

She stressed that her department was strongly opposed to the "commercialization" of babies. Those adoptions usually resulted in unhappiness because commercial farms paid little or no attention to the condition of the children, she said. They care little about whether the baby is mentally or physically sound and have no idea if the child will be compatible with its new parents. Potter explained that some couples were so eager to adopt that they, too, gave little consideration to those factors, even though they would not "buy a refrigerator or an automobile" without a guarantee. Babies usually don't show deficiencies at birth, Potter said, and knowing nothing about the background of the child, couples would have no idea how it was likely to turn out.

Birth certificates were extremely important when applying for U.S. citizenship, and she urged couples who had already adopted babies to "regularize" them for the sake of the child. Most of the illegal adoptions that Dr. Potter discovered involved couples in Essex County, New Jersey, a state claiming to have one of the most strictly enforced adoption laws in the country.

Canadian child-welfare officials were also expressing concern over the illegal adoptions. Nora Lea, an official of the Canadian Welfare Council in Toronto, noted: "All too many children were being smuggled into the U.S...." British Columbia's superintendent of Child Welfare, Ruby McKay, also had examined Canada's poor policies relating to out-of-country adoptions.

> The placement of Canadian children in American homes, which have not been approved by the State Welfare Department, has earned for Canada a doubtful reputation across the line as to adoption practices. As many of the homes used in this type of placement are homes that have been rejected by the social agencies in the United States, it would be well if each province could establish policies with Canadian and American Immigration Departments, and also pass legislation prohibiting agencies from advertising children for adoption.

To avoid an even bigger scandal, child-welfare officials in Canada and the U.S. advised immigration officials to be on the lookout for the unauthorized movement of adopted babies. New Jersey legislators then imposed a ban on all adoptions that did not have government approval. Officials there said they wanted to "safeguard the child" and help both the birth mothers and the adopting parents. Ellen Potter placed an advertisement in a newspaper notifying people of the illegal adoptions and reported that communications between her department and Canadian authorities had resulted in closer surveillance of adoption agencies.

Lila and William, always one step ahead, merely devised an alternative strategy, effective but heartless. They convinced the birth mothers to travel with their babies by train to the U.S. Authorities rarely questioned the mothers, and the infants gained entry on the mothers' passports. In the United States, the mothers handed over their babies to the adoptive parents and returned to Nova Scotia on the next train. Lila and William convinced the mothers to agree to the arrangement as a means of seeing for themselves that their babies were going into good homes. The Youngs thus bypassed the requirement for visas. If the new parents wished, they could legalize the adoption in a surrogate court in the U.S.

Health Minister Davis was unable to stop mothers from taking their babies into the U.S., but he did attempt to stop American couples from coming to Nova Scotia for babies. Lawyer Charles Longley recalled an American couple awaiting the finalization of an adoption. The baby's mother could not support the child and was unable to obtain financial help from the government, so she had placed the baby for adoption. Just as the American couple was about to take the baby, Davis stepped in and told them the adoption was illegal because it had not been approved by government. He had the baby removed from the Maternity Home and placed in a foster home in Halifax. Longley, who had arranged the adoption, was told by an official in Davis's department that he could not retrieve the infant unless he paid $150 — the cost of boarding the child at the foster home. Longley made the payment, but authorities still refused to release the baby.

Longley was furious. "This was a very nice couple more than capable of raising a child, and the Consul-General's office had approved the transfer of the baby into the United States. I should have taken the case to court, I could have gunned it out… on a habeas corpus, I'm sure, but I didn't. I chickened out because I knew that the press would pump it up and make a big fuss by saying somebody was trying to take away nice Nova Scotia babies. I wished the rest of my life I had challenged that. If I had had any guts I would have."

Even under the intense scrutiny of authorities in two countries, the Youngs continued to take in girls and surreptitiously arrange adoptions. Girls who had difficulty paying their bills were hounded by the Youngs and often threatened with "police action." Lila's letters to the girls were usually laced with heavy-handed threats, while William's were more cordial.

Freda MacLaren of Halifax wrote to William in January 1946, explaining her difficulty.

> *Am very sorry to have neglected things this way, but due to a streak of sickness this winter was the only reason. And I certainly did appreciate your kindness when I needed your help. But the thing is Doctor, I've had so many bills for my own health that I find it impossible to meet the whole bill and want to know if it would be alright if I made it in a few payments. I know it's not the way I promised, but I could't see what was ahead of me then. Hoping to hear from you soon.*

William wrote back and expressed sympathy for her illness before suggesting she pay her bill even if it meant borrowing the money from relatives or a finance company. The letter was sent on February 1, 1946.

> *Your letter states that you are desirous of getting terms for the*

payment of your account in full. This is not according to our usual form of business, as you are well aware, and you did not state in your letter the terms that you could meet. However, I would like to make the following suggestion to you. Why not go to some relative or friend, and place your full confidence in them, and if they are in no position to help you outright, if they have an established home or other real estate, you could get them to back a loan for you. I would suggest you try to get this loan from the Maritime Finance Limited at Halifax, then you could pay them back in more liberal terms, which we cannot give you. If this can't be done, or you cannot get sufficient backing by some reliable person, then I ask that you write us telling what terms you could meet at this time. Hoping this suggestion will be both a help and blessing to you an awaiting further word from you,
I am
Faithfully yours,
Dr. Wm. P. Young.

Freda's letter was stamped with the number 803, indicating the official number of babies born at the Home since they were required to keep a register in 1940.

Chapter 16

Surviving Court

Despite the absence of an operating licence, William and Lila still accepted requests for babies as the potential profits were simply too enticing. They could pocket up to $10,000 for each baby, but the stepped-up scrutiny by government made it increasingly difficult to move the children into the U.S. As their income dwindled, legal bills escalated. In 1946, William and Lila spent almost as much time in court as they did placing babies for adoption. They were hounded by charges specifically designed to drive them out of business. They were arraigned in the County Magistrate's Court in March on seven charges.

1) Unlawfully boarding a child under 12 without proper consent from the Director of Child Welfare.
2) Unlawfully advertising babies in the newspaper.
3) Operating without a licence.
4) Unlawfully boarding mothers and infants for profit.
5) Unlawful use of the title Doctor, by William.
6-7) Unlawfully practising medicine in Nova Scotia when both Lila and William were not registered on the medical register, contrary to provisions of the Medical Act.

Soon after the charges were laid, the government again amended the Maternity Boarding House Act, giving F.R. MacKinnon even tighter control over the adoption business. The amendments increased the penalties for violations. Each violation could now be considered a separate offence and subject to a $100 fine or fifty days in jail.

On Wednesday, March 27, just weeks after their arraignment, the Youngs returned to the County Police Court to face the charges. After hearing the evidence, Judge R.J. Flinn found them guilty on two counts of operating without a licence, and for unlawfully boarding mothers and babies for profit. The five remaining charges were either thrown out, withdrawn or adjourned. William and Lila paid a $50 fine for each conviction.

A month later they were in court again before R.J. Flinn, to answer the charge that William was illegally practising medicine and using the title doctor. Four witnesses testified for the prosecution. Two former residents of the Home — Stella Melong, a practical nurse, and Catherine Keating, a graduate nurse from the Halifax Infirmary Hospital — had been at the Maternity Home in the mid-1940s. Keating told the court that Lila supervised the administration of anesthetics. "Mr. Young was never in the case room except to assist in removing patients after deliveries," she said. "He had nothing to do with the patients — his job was to handle the business end of the institution." Nurse Keating said while she worked at the Home, a medical doctor was never in the delivery room

A mother, not publicly identified, testified that she saw William wearing a white coat in the delivery room while her baby was being born, but her evidence was discredited when she admitted she was under the influence of chloroform at the time and could not remember exactly what had taken place. Another unidentified mother said she had also seen William in a white coat in the delivery room. On completion of her testimony, the case was adjourned for a month.

When they returned to County Court in May, two defence witnesses took the stand: William and Lila Young. "William is a chiropractor and a medical missionary," said Lila in a surly tone. "He never pretended to be a medical practitioner." Lila said William rarely examined patients, and she usually did any blood testing. William followed his wife to the stand and explained that he occasionally filled in case-history sheets, but never delivered babies. After hearing the evidence, Judge Flinn dismissed the charge against William. "I've got to consider the evidence, not my own ideas and the ideas of the Crown on what was going on in this institution," he said.

Judge Flinn then heard evidence on the charge that Lila was practising medicine without a licence. Lila took the stand in her own defence, saying that after six years of study from medical books and one year of internship in a Chicago hospital, she obtained a diploma from the National College of Obstetrics and Midwifery. She said that she had handled between 800 and 900 deliveries at the Ideal Maternity Home and "lost only two mothers," one of whom was attended to by two doctors. "The only question is whether she went beyond the duties of a midwife to practice medicine," Judge Flinn said at the end of the day. He would assess the evidence and deliver his verdict at a later date.

Because of the Youngs' high profile during the election campaign, newspapers paid close attention to William and Lila through their many court appearances. On June 5, the Halifax *Herald* headline read: "Fines Levied In Home Case." William and Lila had been found guilty of illegally adopting four babies to U.S. couples. F.R. MacKinnon reported that the Youngs notified his department about the adoptions, but he had not given his consent.

William tried to convince the judge the girls arranged the adoptions themselves, but Judge Flinn did not accept his defence. A letter sent to one of the mothers, signed by William, was produced by Crown Prosecutor W.C. Dunlop: "Your child has been placed for adoption in a home above reproach. If you knew these people, I am certain that you would be as elated as we are."

Even after repeated questioning on procedures, William maintained the mothers had arranged the adoptions. Declaring the story preposterous, Judge Flinn demanded to know how "this baby was let out for adoption before the mother even knew the people." When William's lawyer, R. Clifford Levy, objected to the line of questioning, Judge Flinn shouted, "As counsel for the Home, you should be astute enough to see that this orgy of perjury is stopped!"

The prosecutor then briefed the jury on the adoption of David Hartling, born at the Maternity Home in November 1945. His birth mother, Ethel, was living in Jeddore on the eastern shore of Nova Scotia and worked in Halifax as a domestic. After the birth of her baby in Halifax, Ethel took him to the Ideal Maternity Home and paid the Youngs $350 for his adoption. Ethel never met Ben and Edna Levinson, who eventually adopted her child. This created difficulties for William on the stand. Usually staid and serious, William became furious under pressure. His eyes bulged and saliva flew as he stuttered and provided inconsistent information. Initially, he told Crown Prosecutor Dunlop that he could not recall meeting the Levinsons:

"How did the baby become adopted by the Levinsons?" Dunlop asked.

"Do you want to know?" William replied.

"Yes," said Dunlop.

"You use my right title and you will find out. You address me as doctor and you will find out."

"How did these people get the child?"

"They came to the institution."

"Was there consent from [a] Children's Aid Society?"

"No."

"Or the Director of Child Welfare?"

"Application was made, but consent was never received."

The judge found the Youngs guilty of the charges and handed them the maximum fine under the law: $400 — $100 for each illegal adoption. They had to pay legal costs as well, totaling $28.90. Defence lawyer R. Clifford Levy gave notice that he would appeal the convictions to a higher court. He argued that the notices of adoptions filed with the director were sufficient under the Maternity Boarding House Act.

The appeal was heard in September 1946, before Mr.

Justice K.R. Crowell. William took the stand and, referring to previous hearings, asked the prosecutor, "Why don't you say I was persecuted as well as prosecuted?" He testified that one of the babies adopted by a Jewish couple in New York was three months old when it was brought to the Home. The mother had signed papers asking the Youngs to arrange the adoption. We charged the mother $350, William said, because the baby was in the Home for a month and twenty-four days before being adopted.

F.R. MacKinnon stated that he had not given consent for the adoptions. The judge accepted his testimony and upheld the earlier conviction. Levy, in a final attempt to win something for his clients, argued, to no effect, that the fines were exorbitant as his clients were not attempting to evade the law.

William and Lila were also winning a few cases. The earlier charge that the Youngs were illegally advertising the adoption of babies was thrown out when the Youngs' lawyer produced a letter from the files at the Halifax *Herald*. The letter, written by an unidentified Public Health Department official, authorized the printing of the advertisements. The charge that Lila was practising medicine without a licence was also dismissed for lack of evidence.

A charge of perjury against William stuck. It was placed by Judge R.J. Flinn and Crown Prosecutor W.C. Dunlop, who were annoyed with William's insolence on the witness stand during the June 1946 trial on illegal adoptions. They accused him of lying when he claimed that Rose Agnes Brown arranged for the adoption of her son, Roderick Joseph Brown, at the Home in the fall of 1945.

Rose Brown had just begun to put her upsetting experience behind her when she was subpoenaed to testify at a preliminary hearing in November 1946. She was the Crown's key witness against William. In the earlier trial, it had been established that Rose was not even in the Home when Jack and Bertha Greenberg came to adopt her baby. At the preliminary hearing, Rose said that she had signed documents giving

William permission to adopt her baby.

"It was left there for adoption?" asked Dunlop.

"Yes," Rose replied.

"You paid for it?"

"Yes."

"Have you seen the child since?"

"No, and I don't want to."

"Do you know a man by the name of Jack Greenberg?"

"No."

Dunlop grabbed two documents from his desk — a transfer agreement and a power of attorney contract — and placed them before Rose.

"Did you see documents such as these while you were at the institution or did you sign one like that?"

"I have seen all those, but I never read them over. I signed the papers, but I never read them."

"Did you sign a paper such as this while you were there?"

"I don't remember."

"Were you given such a paper?"

"I don't remember."

In an unusual move, Judge Flinn took the stand himself to testify against William. He told the court William claimed he had had "nothing to do with the adoptions." The judge ruled there was enough evidence to send William to trial in March 1947, in Nova Scotia's Supreme Court. The presiding judge, Mr. Justice John Doull, was the same man who presided at the Eva Nieforth manslaughter trial more than a decade earlier. William, represented by R. Clifford Levy, pleaded not guilty.

Because of lengthy questioning by Levy and Crown Prosecutor Dunlop, the selection of the twelve-man jury was slow. It was difficult to find people who did not know of the Youngs or did not have an opinion on the controversial adoption business. Once a jury was impanelled, the Crown called four witnesses: Judge Flinn; court reporter Mary Feron; William's secretary, Jean Feader; and the child's mother, Rose Brown.

Rose restated that she had not been at the Ideal Maternity Home the previous March when an American couple came to adopt her baby. She said she had never seen the couple or had any correspondence with them. Rose told the jury she had signed over power of attorney to William.

Jean Feader told the court she had worked at the Home from January 1945 until June 1946 and that part of her job was to take care of the adoption papers. She was asked if she had written the letter telling Rose her child had been adopted by "a grand U.S. couple."

"I imagine I did," Feader said. "I couldn't say for sure. It wasn't dictated."

"Were you told to write it?" asked the prosecutor.

"I was."

William did not testify. In fact, there was not a single defence witness, yet to the shock and disbelief of the courtroom, jury foreman David Moulton announced a not-guilty verdict. Mr. Justice John Doull was outraged: "How twelve men could not find him guilty I don't know."

Defiant as ever, the Youngs continued sending out price lists and brochures, which gave no hint of their ordeal: "Many elaborate homes in this world are merely houses without the prattle and play of children in them to add joy and happiness. If yours is a childless home, or if you have been entrusted with means and ability, why not adopt a lovely baby from the Ideal Maternity Home."

Being dragged through the courts might have harmed their reputation, but the Youngs were determined to carry on maintaining their smooth, confident veneer — and their ruthless determination beneath the surface. Elizabeth Anne Harriman, a young woman from Moncton, New Brunswick, gave birth to a girl at the Maternity Home in January 1947. The Youngs did not permit Elizabeth to breast-feed her baby, and two days after the birth, while she was still in a highly delicate state, William Young insisted she sign adoption papers. William urged her to falsify the documents by stating that the father of her baby was Jewish. If she did not sign within fourteen days of the baby's birth, William told her, she would be charged another $30. The young mother later said if she had been allowed to nurse, she probably would not have signed the transfer agreement.

With her baby's adoption documents signed, William felt he had the authority to place Elizabeth Harriman's baby. The Youngs were contacted by an American couple wanting to adopt it, but with F.R. MacKinnon and others watching so closely, they did not know how they could discretely get the infant across the border. When Lila discovered the baby's birth father was a member of the Royal Canadian Mounted Police, she insisted he obtain a police rubber stamp from his office and use it to certify the passport application. The officer refused to comply, and the adoption fell through. Elizabeth Harriman's baby died at the Ideal Maternity Home six months later and was buried in a butterbox. Lila's letter to the RCMP officer, dated January 17, 1947, would later be used in court as evidence against the Youngs.

The supply of babies, the constant demand of well-to-do couples seeking to adopt, and the Youngs' greed and contempt for the law proved too much for Davis and MacKinnon and their provincial regulations. But the Youngs would be less successful against the intensely negative publicity outside Nova Scotia. It was triggered in Montreal by a newspaper reporter named Mavis Gallant, who, in later years, went on to become one of Canada's best known authors internationally and was a recipient of the Order of Canada in 1981.

Chapter 17

Traders in Fear

William and Lila's court cases attracted local media attention, but the Ideal Maternity Home became a national spectacle after a visit by a Nova Scotia freelance writer, David MacLellan, in June 1946. Midway through their many court appearances, they gave MacLellan a tour of the institution. He thought the layout was adequate, but he noticed an "unclean hospital smell. And it was crowded. A lot of people were running in and out of the kitchen." Eighteen pregnant women were in the Home. Lila explained to MacLellan that each paid between $300 and $500 for the delivery and adoption of the baby. Lila said she had delivered 877 babies at the Home. MacLellan met a Jewish musician and his wife from the United States, who were waiting to adopt a baby. MacLellan understood that with power of attorney the Youngs could proceed with the adoption. The couple was assured there would be no publicity.

Lila and William told MacLellan that they had been hounded and persecuted by the courts and the government, and dragged into court on twenty-three occasions. Before leaving, MacLellan noticed a large quantity of chinaware unpacked in the laboratory and a microscope covered with dust. William and Lila told him they were preparing to close the Maternity Home and open a hotel.

MacLellan sold his information to *The Standard*, a weekly newspaper based in Montreal with a national circulation. Mavis Gallant, a twenty-four-year-old staff writer, had been hired by the newspaper during the war years, when there was a shortage of male reporters. She pleaded with her editors to send her to Nova Scotia as part of her investigation of the Home,

The (*Montreal*) Standard,
August 31, 1946.

Traders In Fear
Baby farm rackets still lure girls who are afraid of social agencies
By Mavis Gallant

but they refused, saying they could not spare the time or the expense. Gallant, therefore, never met William and Lila Young but verified the facts of her story by letter and long-distance telephone.

Days before Gallant's story was published, William and Lila opened their new business, Young's Hotel and Rest Home, which they advertised as "a delightful surrounding for tired business people and the aged." They called their new establishment the Battle Creek of Nova Scotia — Rest Haven Park. "We'll be looking after those who are getting ready to leave this world, instead of those who are coming into it," Lila said. A letter sent to the Youngs shortly after the opening revealed the amount elderly people were paying to stay there.

> *In consideration of the care offered our mother Mrs. Mary Barton at the Young's Hotel and Rest Home, we promise payment of her care there at a rate of four dollars a day ($120 per month) payable monthly, in advance.*

"Baby farm rackets still lure girls who are afraid of social agencies." This bold red headline splashed across the front page of *The Standard* promoted Mavis Gallant's exposé of the Ideal Maternity Home. Published on August 31, 1946, the story featured an idyllic photograph of fourteen healthy-looking babies all about one year old. Bunched together on a blanket spread out on the lawn in front of the East Chester maternity home, four women, one in a nurse's uniform, cuddled some of the infants. Gallant wrote,

> To hundreds of girls in trouble the Ideal Maternity Home in East Chester looked like a good bet. It offered what seemed the most important thing to an unmarried mother: adequate care and not too many questions. But the frightened young women who flocked there from all over Canada signed away everything from their life's savings to their babies, without a murmur.

Gallant reported that by the time the girls paid their full hotel rates and the adoption charges, the amount often came to $500. She condemned the contracts giving William Young power of attorney.

> Through fear, ignorance and the desire for anonymity, they didn't realize what it would mean. Many of them regretted having signed away their baby while they were in a worried, irrational state. But they couldn't do a thing — especially if the child had been adopted by people of no stated address.

Gallant referred to the charges resulting from the placement of Protestant babies in Jewish homes. "The religious angle was not the main issue," she wrote, "but it gave the welfare authorities something to worry about as all agencies, both Jewish and non-Jewish, had a strict practice of placing Protestant, Catholic and Jewish children in homes of the same faith,"

The report suggested there was nothing unusual about

the Ideal Maternity Home; it was "just a little more blatant" than most. The "little nest" of privately run maternity homes did not advertise extensively the way the Youngs did. Most were known by their reputations. "Why do mothers go to baby farms, private maternity homes and other black market sources?" Gallant asked.

> According to social workers, it is because they have a traditional prejudice against agencies and are afraid the social workers will contact their families or write to people in their towns. Self-styled maternity homes thrive on this sort of fear and ignorance. Though the mother might regret losing her child through an illegal agency, the greatest hardship, of course, was felt by the child.

"It would be wrong to say the situation isn't getting any better," Gallant wrote facetiously. "Every once in a while the authorities catch up with someone, fine them a stiff $12.50 or so, and give them a good scolding. The Youngs of East Chester weren't the least bit discouraged by their setbacks in court. They're entering a new enterprise: a home for the aged."

Gallant's article did not deal with suspicions of baby trafficking, and it did not explore the neglect and high death rate among babies, yet when it hit the newspaper stands, it shook an entire community. Seventy-seven thousand copies of the weekly were distributed in the Maritime Provinces. People involved directly or indirectly with the adoptions business scrambled to distance themselves from the Youngs. The scandal pervaded the Maritimes, and the solid support the Youngs once enjoyed began to crumble. Former admirers who had depicted Lila and William as humanitarians devoted to their "labour of love" suddenly saw them as opportunists, lining their pockets by selling babies and fleecing both destitute young mothers and generous supporters.

The Nova Scotia government was uncomfortable having its dirty laundry aired before a national audience. "The Home was an embarrassment," F.R. MacKinnon recalls. "It had become too big and very obvious. It was a *cause célèbre*, a very large facility in a very small community. Had it remained small it wouldn't have created such public excitement. It was a black mark on the province."

The exploitation of unwed mothers and their babies was likely not the sole reason for national interest in the Ideal Maternity Home. Gallant was assigned the story at a time when the role of midwives was being officially challenged by the country's powerful male-dominated medical profession. There was a movement afoot to do away with midwives altogether. The Canadian Medical Association had resolved that physicians should take full responsibility for the delivery of babies. By 1947, midwifery was nearly wiped out in many Canadian provinces. More than two decades passed before women of the 1970s began to effectively question the social and psychological shortcomings of medical births and midwifery resurfaced as a valuable alternative.

After Gallant's article, Nova Scotia officials received numerous telephone calls from child welfare officials throughout Canada and the U.S. asking about the legitimacy of the Home. "We never knew what to tell them," MacKinnon says, "because we didn't have any control over the adoptions."

William and Lila were incensed, arguing that the accusations were false and that their reputation as honest business people had suffered irreparable harm. They sued the Montreal Standard Publishing Company for $25,000.

Early on the morning of May 9, 1947, William and Lila strode stoically into the old Halifax courthouse, an eighty-five-year-old sandstone structure in south-end Halifax, flanked by lawyers F.W. Bissett of Halifax and R. Clifford Levy of Chester. Their long-time legal advisor, Charles Longley, had refused to handle the libel case.

Longley had been opposed to suing *The Standard* because he felt it would be a ruinous action. Not only would the Youngs lose, but they would also destroy whatever reputa-

William and Lila Young sued The Standard *for libel after it published a front page story about the Home.*

tions they had left. He told William and Lila that the newspaper would get some high-powered lawyers and they would end up in the position of defendants. In Longley's words, "Everybody would hate their guts, and make them look like miserable slimeballs." The Youngs failed to see the wisdom in Longley's advice and doggedly pursued the libel suit. "They asked me to help them find another lawyer," Longley recalls. "I recommended F.W. Bissett of Halifax, who later became a judge of the Nova Scotia Supreme Court." But Longley pessimistically maintained that no lawyer could win this case. "It was doomed from the beginning."

The publishing company's high-powered lawyers were Harry P. MacKeen, KC, of Halifax, Nova Scotia's most renowned criminal lawyer of the day, who later became Lieutenant-Governor (1963–1968), and W. Pitt Potter, KC, of Lunenburg, a tall, stern figure known for his keen mind and sharp wit, who later became a judge of the Federal Court of

Canada. The Halifax courtroom was about to become a battleground for some of the top legal minds in the province with William and Lila Young at the centre of it all.

The trial was held in the Supreme Court chamber before Mr. Justice W.L. Hall, highly respected for his efforts to develop social work as a profession. Justice Hall helped to establish the Maritime School of Social Work in 1940 and served on a royal commission studying mentally disabled children. He was partially responsible for the establishment of the Nova Scotia Training School for Mentally Retarded Children in 1927. Anyone knowing this formidable figure was aware of his deep appreciation of the plight of unfortunate children, and before this trial was over, his personal view of the Youngs' adoption business would be well known.

On the opening morning, nine men filed into the jurors' box; for most of them, it was their first glimpse of William and Lila Young. During the four days that followed, it would be the job of these nine jurors to determine if Mavis Gallant had her facts right and if the Youngs' reputation was unfairly lowered in the community because of her article. They had to decide whether the story was "fair comment" and whether it was justified. Reporters and spectators jostled for space on crowded wooden benches. Coverage of the trial was extensive, with almost verbatim testimony filling the pages of *The Halifax Mail* and other newspapers.

During the first two days the prosecution called five witnesses: Barry Van Alstyne, the Maritimes circulation representative for *The Standard*; Phyllis Hingley, a Truro woman who had worked for the Youngs; Otto B. Hubley, a Chester poultry farmer; Henry Irving Fraser of the New Brunswick Barristers' Association; and the key prosecution witness, Lila Coolen Young. William Young was conspicuously absent from the prosecution's list, but no reason was speculated upon at the time.

Barry Van Alstyne confirmed that *The Standard*, containing Mavis Gallant's article, had been circulated in Newfoundland and the Maritimes. Phyllis Hingley said that she had been

The Standard *article was written by Mavis Gallant, a young journalist who went on to become one of Canada's best known authors internationally and was awarded the Order of Canada.*

employed by the Youngs as a practical nurse, not a registered nurse, between 1944 and 1947. She worked in the nurseries and did domestic work in the Home. She started work there at the age of nineteen. On an average day, she said, there were thirty mothers and eighty to ninety babies to look after.

Under cross-examination, Hingley admitted that she often saw children with eye infections, colds and pneumonia. Potter asked: "Is it not true that once they reached eighteen months old they were not taken outdoors at all?" "I don't know," said Hingley. When asked what happened to the babies who died, she said she did not know that, either. She had not attended any funerals and was unable to say whether their bodies were buried in butterboxes. Hingley claimed she had never even been in the Home when a baby died. She then denied owing the Youngs money. Later, defence lawyer Harry MacKeen said Hingley was not a believable witness because she "looked terrified of Mrs. Young."

Testimony from another prosecution witness, Otto R. Hubley, was ruled inadmissible. He was to have been a character witness for the Youngs, but Justice Hall said his evidence would only be needed if the defence later introduced evidence of poor character. Henry Irving Fraser, a member of the New Brunswick Bar, was asked by Pitt Potter why he referred to William Young as Dr. Young. Fraser said he had heard William called that by members of the Young family.

While the prosecution witnesses testified, Lila, seated beside William, appeared confident, almost aloof, as she listened to the evidence. When called upon to testify, she maintained her composure throughout several hours of intense questioning. She told the jury she had met William twenty-two years earlier when he was a Seventh-day Adventist minister. She explained that she had studied from her brother's medical books and later received a diploma from a Chicago college. "Why have you never registered as a nurse in Nova Scotia?" Potter asked. "It's beneath my dignity to register as a nurse in Nova Scotia," she said. Lila felt she was automatically licensed for the practice of midwifery by virtue of her Chicago diploma. In her hand she held a framed duplicate of the diploma she had received from the Chicago college; it was stamped "The West End Hospital."

In an effort to discredit her, the mercurial Pitt Potter handed her a telegram. The courtroom was silent as she read aloud, "The West End Hospital — closed in 1931 — never on the accredited list of the American Medical Association, and the American Medical Association never recognized midwifery." Lila, unflappable, downplayed the significance of the telegram, proceeding as if it did not exist.

When Pitt Potter asked about the contents of *The Standard's* story, Lila maintained that "*The Standard* had lied," and when previous court cases were mentioned, "justice had a miscarriage," said Lila winking at her lawyers.

After Lila explained the fee system, Potter wanted to know why the cost was so high. Lila said "some of the girls were charged more than $300 if we had to feed them for very long. Some worked off their bills, others, she said, ran away without paying."

Midway through her lengthy testimony, Lila looked at the nine male jurors and made an impassioned plea. "I thought of the Home as a sanctuary for the mothers. We didn't charge all the girls. There were many charity cases. The girls were given fictitious names, but their correct names were always put in the register. The mothers signed the adoption papers without a murmur. We wouldn't have had it any other way. The institution was always clean, and as for professional help, we were never without because there were always four or five nurses waiting to be confined."

Lila explained that during her eighteen years in East Chester she had delivered 890 babies, but she could not provide any records to show how many lived and how many had died. "So you brought babies into the world, you passed them around in the world, and you buried them," Potter said. "I certainly did," she answered. When Potter asked if she had documents showing she was a registered undertaker, she said tersely, "Anyone who lays out the dead is an undertaker."

Potter paced the floor directly in front of the witness box, stopped suddenly, and shouted: "Didn't you make money on children who died after the mother had already paid $300 to cover the adoption?" Lila explained that in many cases the money was refunded.

Before leaving the stand at 1:25 p.m. on day two of the trial, Lila delivered her parting shot. When Potter asked about infants sent to Jewish families in the United States, Lila seemed delighted to have the opportunity to once again malign her old foe, Frank Davis. "Some of the children of Christian parents were placed with Jewish families in the States," she said. "The provincial Health minister set the precedent for this when [through a public agency] he placed a child with a Dr. Susman of Staten Island." Potter ended his cross-examination with Lila looking smug.

On the afternoon of day two, Harry MacKeen and Pitt Potter launched a two-pronged defence, asserting that the article was substantially true and it was fair comment. Called to testify was F.R. MacKinnon; Dr. Barrie Coward; freelance writer David MacLellan; the Deputy Registrar of Joint Stock companies, Doug Sutherland; Elizabeth Harriman, a mother; and another mother, not publicly identified, who had stayed at the Home. Mavis Gallant was not asked to appear. Clearly, the defence saw David MacLellan as the main contributor to

The Standard article. He took the stand first, testifying briefly about his visit to the Home. He described his tour through the Home, then told the court that the Youngs said they had been hauled into court on twenty-three different occasions, a comment Lila had earlier denied making.

Doug Sutherland, Deputy Registrar of Joint Stock Companies for Nova Scotia, told the court the Home was registered in the late 1940s as the Battle Creek of Nova Scotia — Rest Haven Park. The Home's certificate of incorporation was still valid in 1947.

When Child Welfare Director F.R. MacKinnon took the stand and testified that he had studied social welfare at the University of Chicago, MacKeen asked, "Is that a recognized university? There's some question about these Chicago institutions." MacKinnon, smiling, replied, "It is." MacKinnon told the court about the inspections at the Home on August 6 and October 3, 1945, and outlined the unsatisfactory conditions. "Compared with two other institutions, the Home of the Guardian Angel and the Halifax Infants' Home, conditions at this institution were inferior. They did not meet recognized health or nutritional standards. Under cross-examination, MacKinnon explained his reason for refusing the Youngs a licence: "I had made a number of recommendations for improvement at the institution which were ignored. The system used to place children would have been enough to refuse a licence."

MacKinnon was asked if he had said that he hoped the peddling of illegitimate children in Nova Scotia was over as a result of the Home closing. He admitted making the comment and he added that he thought the use of the word "peddling" was appropriate. He considered the Home's admission fees alone "sufficient justification for the use of the term."

Dr. Barrie Coward, described as an expert witness, then took the stand. Mr. Justice Hall smiled and laughter erupted in the courtroom when Harry MacKeen mistakenly introduced him as Noel Coward. Dr. Coward corroborated MacKinnon's assessment of the October 3 inspection at the Home. "The overcrowding was striking," he said, "and nutrition was very poor. The babies were in poor health." Dr. Coward outlined Lila's feeding schedule, arranged according to age. "On the whole, conditions were unsatisfactory."

He mentioned the fly-filled nurseries and the poor condition of the babies. There were quite a few cases of illness and red buttocks, he said. Dr. Coward also reported on the babies he had examined before they were adopted. Their health was poor, but he admitted he had rejected only one infant as unfit for adoption, and that was because of a physical defect. He did not elaborate. Dr. Coward acknowledged that other "hospitals" also suffered from a shortage of help, but he said they at least took the babies into the open air when they were confined for any length of time.

The defence lawyers had difficulty getting mothers to testify. They had hoped their stay at the Home would be the "last chapter," MacKeen explained. Only two agreed to appear. An unidentified mother said her baby had died at the Home six days after birth and had not received medical care at any point. She said she was in the Home when at least one other baby became sick and died. No doctor was called in then either. She remembered its burial in a butterbox. She then admitted that she had been asked by the Youngs to pose as a nurse during inspections and that there was much "hurry and scurry" when the inspectors arrived.

Elizabeth Harriman, the second mother, was later described by the judge as "someone who told her story absolutely fairly." She delivered damning testimony, telling the jury that after her baby was born, William asked her to falsify the transfer agreement by stating that the father of the baby was Jewish. William apparently knew of a couple in the U.S. wanting to adopt a Jewish child. Elizabeth told the court that Lila had taken extreme measures to get the baby's father to use an RCMP rubber stamp on a passport. A letter written by Lila, later described by MacKeen as a request for "just a little forgery," was introduced as evidence.

This brief note is being sent to Miss Harriman with the request that she pass it to you personally to avoid all possible publicity in this case and I will try to make it clear what we want you to do and why.

As you will see by the enclosed application of a passport, the baby born to your friend has been placed for adoption in a magnificent home in the United States where it will receive the utmost care, love and affection, and every advantage in life. But to get the child over the border into the United States she must have a passport and this passport must be certified by a mayor or notary or physician, or police officer.

We do not want to take any more persons into the circle of knowing of this child than can be avoided and since you are a police officer, and since there is no way of identifying you with the birth of this child by your certifying that you have known Miss Harriman for a year, we think it best that you sign the enclosed application as a voucher where I have marked an X with your position in the RCMP.

You need not bring the matter to your superior officer but simply sign it and fill in your address, rank etc. If you have access to an RCMP *rubber stamp, it would be excellent to stamp it. Then please put it in the mail immediately as time is a factor without a place here to keep the baby and the folks want her as soon as they can.*

I think I have made this real clear to you, except that when you receive it PLEASE DO IT AT ONCE *and as soon as it is in the mail please drop a line to your friend Miss Harriman in my care, telling when it was completed and posted so we will know how to judge time in making appointments for plane and with the Consul etc. etc.*

Thanking you for your kind and prompt attention and assuring you of our utmost help and co-operation I am,
Faithfully Yours,
Lila Coolen Young, Obstetrician

Elizabeth Harriman's testimony likely discredited the Youngs more than any other. In a brilliant finale on the fourth day, defence lawyer Harry MacKeen did exactly what Charles Longley had predicted. In defending the newspaper, he effectively prosecuted the Youngs. Recapping the stinging testimony against William and Lila, he said, "This case we've been trying in the past few days marks an all-time high. These chronic law-breakers are seeking damages for a reputation they did not possess." He suggested the jury might have been puzzled about why the trial was held in Halifax instead of Lunenburg County, the Youngs' home. "There is only one answer to that," MacKeen said. "They are known in Lunenburg. If they had a good reputation in that county, they would have filed the lawsuit there."

MacKeen maintained that *The Standard* article was fair, that a writer could use "ridicule, sarcasm and irony" as long as he did not use them unfairly. Days before the story was published, the Home closed, he said, so the Youngs "didn't lose one cent" from the negative publicity. He contended that the institution was in violation of the law throughout its eighteen years in business. "The law was designed for the protection of the unfortunate children who might go to the Home. How did the Youngs know those babies weren't being taken to the United Sates for the purpose of blackmailing the fathers?"

MacKeen noted that William Young chose not to testify. "Instead he stood behind the ample skirts of his wife. And there's the 'doctor' title he basks under. Why do you think that is used? It's to make ignorant, unfortunate girls believe they are being treated by a medical doctor."

The practice of getting mothers to sign away their children "before they learned to love them" was cruel, MacKeen said, and he called the methods used to collect money "unforgivable." He referred to a letter written by William to one of the mothers who left the Home without paying her bill in which police action was threatened. "If there was any question of blackmail," he charged, "there it is." He pointed out that the law did not allow for such threats to collect money. "Deception," he declared, "ran through the entire operation."

> And what about the conditions at the Home? The Youngs had an opportunity to refute comments from a pediatrician and others who inspected the Home but they chose not to. And, although the nursing profession was one of the noblest in the world, Mrs. Young felt it beneath her dignity. The jury, too, must have noticed her sauciness throughout the entire hearing, her unmitigated and patent perjury.

But her level of perjury "sinks into insignificance," MacKeen continued, compared with "one of the most damning frauds ever put over on a young man." MacKeen recalled that when Lila Young was asked if she had ever collected money from a father after the death of his baby, she had replied, "Oh, my Lord, no, I wouldn't think of it. I would be afraid of my soul." At this point Lila, seated alongside her husband, was heard whispering, "That's right, that's right." MacKeen held up two documents before the jury, a birth certificate and a death certificate from the Cyril Covey fraud trial. He then held up a third document signed by Lila, a declaration from the baby's mother. "Did you ever hear of such a barefaced gyp!" MacKeen shouted. "They attempted to rook the father for money for the child when it was dead." He scoffed at Lila's comment that the mother had put her up to it.

MacKeen then described "one of the foulest episodes ever put before the court in its long history of crime and filth." He referred to Elizabeth Harriman, who had testified that William Young had wanted her to sign a statement saying the father of her child was Jewish. The East Chester chiropractor had asked this mother to "falsify the blood" of her own child. "Traders in fear?" he roared. "Traders in blood — traders in deception."

MacKeen was not through. "*The Standard* article was substantially true and was fair comment. We say it is a crusade to frighten unmarried mothers all over Canada to keep clear of these racket shops. We're not ashamed of the story. And what did it accomplish? Mrs. Young told the court she gave up the adoption business when she closed the Home. Yet, after the closure, price lists were sent to prospective clients. And one letter accompanying a price list said she was not interested in any case where adoption was not required. She's still in the same practice," cried MacKeen. "It's business as usual! And was it expensive? There was the $35 burial fee! For what, butter-boxes? The trunk of the Youngs' car? I say it was expensive compared to what a girl would get at an institution like The Infants' Home."

F.W. Bissett could not match MacKeen's brilliance. His evidence against *The Standard* was weak, and, as Justice Hall later said, "perplexing." Standing before the jury with the newspaper in hand, Bissett charged that the story was designed to make readers believe his clients were dishonest people who "victimized, exploited and blackmailed young unmarried mothers." The headline, "Traders in Fear," was clearly defamatory and false, he said. Details of the story had caused serious damage to his clients' reputation. Mavis Gallant's reference to convictions against the Youngs was libelous because they were against the Maternity Home, not the Youngs personally. Lawyer Bissett said he was seeking special damages because his clients suffered a loss of business at their hotel and rest home after the story was published.

But Bissett's case quickly collapsed. His key witness, Lila Young, had been thoroughly discredited; he had been unable to prove a loss of reputation or revenues as a result of the newspaper article. Bissett's weak defence received minimal newspaper coverage.

When Bissett completed his final arguments, at least one person in the public gallery shuddered. Charles Longley had dropped by to check out the trial. "It was difficult to watch," he said later, "because *The Standard's* lawyers Potter and MacKeen outclassed and outmaneuvered Bissett in every way." Longley thought Potter was cagey and had provided a respectable defence for the newspaper. But Potter's colleague, Harry MacKeen, was more impressive. "He was a genius and he knew how to make the most out of the burial practices. I could see the disgust on the faces of the jurors when he talked about the butterboxes. And Lila didn't help matters. On the stand she was trying to be forceful and hold her own, but she wasn't succeeding. She had adopted a belligerent attitude and I could tell she wasn't winning any sympathy from the jury."

On the final day of the trial, Mr. Justice Hall read his charge to the jury, leaving little doubt as to where he stood personally. "The headline 'Traders in Fear' came the closest to libel of anything in the article. But is it libel?" he asked. He described the case as a *cause célèbre* — the subject matter in the story was in the public interest. "It's a matter that affects the social life of the province." Courtrooms, he said, were not large enough to hold the wide audience that had wanted to attend the trial.

"If you deal with fair comment," Judge Hall explained, "you could ask yourself, would any fair man have said what this article said?" The judge noted that the Youngs' lawyer felt the headline was libelous, but they had not claimed libel in the subheading, "Baby farm rackets still lure girls who are afraid of social agencies." Justice Hall read from *The Standard* that 'the girls had regretted signing away their babies.' Do you doubt that? I don't. But I'm not the judge of the facts."

Referring to William's efforts to have a Jewish name placed on a birth certificate, Justice Hall exclaimed, "That's an honest man? This ex-missionary who is claiming damage to his reputation?" He then dealt with the defendants' claim that the Youngs were dishonest by referring to a letter written by Lila within forty-eight hours after the birth of a baby. In the letter she had told the father the child had been placed "in a magnificent home" in the United States. "How did she know at that early date that the baby would go to a magnificent home in the U.S.? It must have been television or something," His Lordship said.

Justice Hall also dealt with Bissett's argument that the

convictions referred to in *The Standard* had been laid against the Home, not against the Youngs personally. "Ah, well, gentlemen," he asked, "whom were the charges against?" He noted the Home was an incorporated company and the Youngs held 1,998 of the two thousand shares. There were only two shares outside the family, and they were held by the directors. "The Youngs owned, operated and managed the business, yet they said they had nothing to do with it?"

He concluded that if the jury found the newspaper article to be true, there could be only one possible verdict, and it would favour *The Standard*. Regarding the five infants who were sent to the United States for adoption, he said, "There's not a word of evidence that any of them were ever adopted. They've gone to God knows where."

On Thursday, May 15, 1947, *The Halifax Mail* headline read: "Twenty-five thousand dollar libel action dismissed in Supreme Court." As Longley had forecast, the court not only favoured the Montreal Standard Publishing Company, but the Youngs had been made to look like criminals. The verdict read by Jury Foreman A. Milton Darrach was delivered after only an hour and twenty minutes of deliberation. A Halifax newspaper reporter wrote: "The portly East Chester midwife ... sat tight-lipped as the verdict was given. Mrs. Young sat with arms folded and received the announcement without comment."

"I'm not going to congratulate you, gentlemen," Mr. Justice Hall concluded, "but I think it is the verdict of an intelligent jury. You will have the consolation of knowing that by your verdict, you have struck another blow at the black market in babies."

Mavis Gallant would have been greatly relieved by the verdict. In a letter to author Bette Cahill sent from her Paris home in 1989, Gallant said could not recall precise details of the story she had reported forty-three years earlier. What she did remember was the treatment she received from her superiors at *The Standard*. Her letter, shown here in part, is an interesting glimpse into a bygone era.

Paris, 26, November 89
Dear Bette Cahill,
The original research was done by a reporter from Nova Scotia … whose name I have forgotten. The Standard did not send me to N.S. — I had to do all my checking, verification from Montreal. When the trial took place, the editors & manager of the paper behaved like frightened rabbits. Their treatment of me (I was twenty-four) was, I still think, despicable.

I had never heard of the story until it was assigned to me, but—I don't quite know how to explain it — a subtle atmosphere was created; the whole mess was my fault. Some people thought I had suggested one story and had through my incompetence led the newspaper into a legal mess. There was no doubt in my mind that had we lost the case I would have been out of a job.

In those days, women were not welcome except on the cooking and fashion pages. We had been hired during the war when there was a shortage of men and during the postwar years we hung on by the skin of our teeth. The lawyers never questioned me, no one asked me for my notes or my file, and when I tried to mention the case I was told to shut up. Had we lost, I'd have been the scapegoat…

…As to why The Standard was interested in a Nova Scotia story: the paper was not a local daily, but a weekly with national distribution. I begged to be sent to Nova Scotia, but they did not want to allow me the time (one travelled by train in those days) or the expense. In fact, I must have spent the equivalent of train fare on long distance calls and as for time needed to write a thorough piece, I always managed …
Yours Sincerely
Mavis Gallant

F.R. MacKinnon never forgot how elated he felt when the trial was over. "It was a time to celebrate. It was one of the happiest days of my life." MacKinnon was in his mid-thirties and on his way to becoming a department head in Nova Scotia Public Welfare when the libel trial ended. "The trial could have gone the other way. We had no way of knowing how each witness would perform on the stand, or what evidence would be presented. The government could have looked silly, but it didn't, and we were pleased." MacKinnon was no doubt relieved that after the trial no one asked the tough question: Why had the government allowed the Youngs to stay in business for more than eighteen years before shutting them down?

F.R. MacKinnon, always cautious not to criticize the way in which Frank Davis handled the Youngs, says if someone less determined than Davis had been in power the Home would have stayed in business longer, perhaps until the late 1950s. In the end it was the butterboxes and baby deaths that destroyed their business. "I truly believe they were laughed out of business," MacKinnon says. "People in Nova Scotia felt abhorrence, distaste, and guilt when they learned of the burial practices. Public opinion turned on them. The media coverage, the many charges and prosecutions finally defeated them."

After the trial, MacKinnon had no further contact with Lila and William and that was fine with him, but he never forgot those early days. "Because of the dynamics between Lila Young and Frank Davis, efforts to close the Home had to end in confrontation," he says. "The business became too uppity, too saucy." Today, MacKinnon draws immense pleasure from the knowledge that he was part of a small but determined group who pioneered laws to protect illegitimate children. "It was an exciting time; we knew we were breaking new ground by making life better for children. Sometimes when I look back, though, I shudder, because even the methods we were using were primitive by today's standards, but it was the best we had at the time. There were no laws protecting illegitimate children, no support for mothers, no restrictions on adoptions, and no laws preventing the sale of human life."

The Youngs survived for so long, MacKinnon says, because they were slick sales people; effective legal counsel also helped. "They weren't sleazy," MacKinnon says. "They were first-rate lawyers who fought their every battle until the end. Benjamin

Guss of Saint John was the district governor of Rotary. To suggest Ben Guss would become involved in anything shady was unthinkable." R. Clifford Levy eventually ended up a minister in Robert Stanfield's cabinet; and Charles Longley, QC, was a partner in the reputable law firm, Longley and Longley.

F.R. MacKinnon carried on the fight to strengthen child welfare laws and in 1959 was appointed Deputy Minister of Public Welfare. He retired from the department in 1980 and instead of fighting for the rights of children went on to become an advocate for the elderly. At eighty, he became the executive director of a provincial cabinet committee called the Senior Citizens' Secretariat.

One of the people closest to Lila and William throughout their years in business, Charles Longley, QC, continued as an adoption lawyer after the Home closed, but he handled far fewer cases than in the early years. His ties with William and Lila were severed after the 1940s. Years later Longley, retired and living in Dartmouth, N.S., recalled those hostile early years in the adoption business and the rift between Lila Young and Frank Davis. "Confrontation and defiance was their way. That Home would probably still be in business today if the Youngs had been willing to comply. We did everything in our power to keep them going... maneuvering around every obstacle. As a lawyer, I had to do what I could to keep my clients in business... legitimately. But in the end they simply refused to accept any advice."

Sixteen months after rejoicing over the outcome of *The Standard* libel trial, Nova Scotia's Public Health minister, Frank Roy Davis, passed away. He suffered a heart attack on September 17, 1948, while attending the annual meeting of the Nova Scotia Medical Society in Ingonish, Cape Breton. Davis's obituary mentioned his heroic rescue work in the 1936 Moose River mine disaster and his many legislative accomplishments, but nowhere was there a reference to his fifteen-year-long battle with The Ideal Maternity Home or his efforts to end the exploitation of illegitimate children in Nova Scotia.

PART IV

Long Shadows
1948–2006

GIVE HIM A CHANCE

18

Bankruptcy

Large-scale baby smuggling all but ended in Nova Scotia after the Ideal Maternity Home officially closed, but less than a year later evidence of a well-established racketeering scheme — not believed to be related to the Youngs — surfaced in neighbouring New Brunswick. On a Thursday night in May 1948, before a packed meeting of the Saint John City and County Children's Aid Society, details of the illegal scheme were revealed. Investigators described how more than fifty babies had been taken from the Saint John area in the previous year. Only a week before this meeting, the Children's Aid Society had "snatched back" five of the babies.

Society officials revealed the inner workings of the baby-selling scheme. Mothers-to-be were solicited by lawyers before their babies were born. The marketing ring paid hospital expenses and gave the mother a cash payment upon birth of the baby, then arranged for its sale. The demand for babies was coming from the United States, and the selling price started at $1,500. Child-welfare investigators did not know how widespread the selling of Canadian babies was, but they suspected it extended to other provinces. The officials urged the province to tighten child-welfare laws so that the commercialization of babies could be stopped.

The following day, F.R. MacKinnon revealed that an unidentified Halifax man was under investigation for the illegal trafficking of babies in Nova Scotia. *The Halifax Mail* quoted MacKinnon in a front-page story: "Although no definite proof so far had been obtainable, strong belief is held that the suspect is messing around in the business. It is suspected there may be private operators or private individuals engaging in placing Nova Scotian babies in the United States." MacKinnon said child-welfare officials were fully aware of the situation. He made no mention of the Youngs or their adoption business, which was still operating illegally — using the hotel as a front — but on a much smaller scale than before.

Following the libel trial, William and Lila began experiencing serious financial problems. Their unforgettable appearance on the political scene, the costs and publicity of the failed libel trial, and widespread skepticism about their moneymaking methods hurt business at their hotel and rest home. To generate income, they held weekly dances. Still claiming to be faithful Seventh-day Adventists, the Youngs did not allow dancing from sundown Friday until sundown Saturday, but after sunset on Saturday evenings the parties were in full swing. The former maternity home already had a reputation as a place to pick up girls, so men travelled great distances to attend. People danced to the bellows and studs of accordion music, and Lila organized contests encouraging people to bid on homemade pies baked by women in the community. The parties often stretched into the early morning hours.

The Youngs also purchased an old ambulance from the air force and attempted to operate a medical emergency service between Halifax and East Chester, but there was not enough demand. Eventually crowds dwindled at their Saturday night dances. When they could no longer afford to pay their taxes or complete renovations, they borrowed money from long-time friend and neighbour Edward Corkum. Initially, they borrowed a sum of money and $2,000 worth of lumber. Edward Corkum was not concerned about the Youngs' inability to repay him immediately. He was a generous man who understood their financial problems and pitied them, according to his son Ray.

William and Lila sank the money into their hotel, which was attracting out of province guests who had no knowledge of its sordid history. In August 1948, an American couple decided to stay a night at Youngs' hotel. Helen and Rafael Blau were on their way to Yarmouth, where Rafael, a former motion-picture writer for Paramount, would work as a freelance writer, and Helen would continue her career as a psychologist.

Rafael recalls their stay. "It was one of the strangest nights of my life, because at first we had no idea these were the people we had read about in the newspapers." Rafael and Helen had hardly settled in when Lila began telling them about her troubles: that her business had been a great success and for no good reason the government shut her down. She pulled out a red-and-black ledger and began flipping through the pages, pointing to the names of babies and the couples who had adopted them. Helen Blau noticed that most of the people were from New Jersey and New York; she also noted a large number of babies' names had "deceased" written beside them.

Just as Helen and Rafael began to realize this was the infamous home they had read about, Lila jumped up and insisted everyone gather around the piano. "I never sang a hymn in my life," Rafael says, but I tried to sing along with her... you know, just mouthing the words."

As Lila played, Rafael kept thinking about the news story of baby deaths and burials in butterboxes. "These people acted as though they were utterly innocent of any wrongdoing. It was like they were salts of the earth — and so self-righteous... as Lila said, she was doing God's work." Rafael and Helen also met William Young. "He was a quiet man, rather pale looking, with a blank stare," Rafael recalls.

William was so quiet that Rafael and his wife learned little about him. They did not discover, for example, that William had established a chiropractic business. From all accounts, William was an able chiropractor, but when he tried to join the Chiropractic Association of Nova Scotia, he was rejected. Former association president George Ibsen had heard about the Youngs' disreputable adoption business and was annoyed that William had been calling himself a doctor and a chiropractor. William had been in Nova Scotia for two decades and had never once tried to establish his credentials. Ibsen claims William could not produce documents verifying that he had graduated from a recognized college.

Ibsen remembers William's visit well, because before leaving his office William showed him a confidential file containing the names of daughters of prominent families who had been sent to the Ideal Maternity Home. Ibsen recalls being surprised at the number of names he recognized. He suspected William frequently used the file as leverage, or possibly blackmail, to get what he wanted.

Rejection from the Chiropractic Association did not discourage William. He continued in business, and some people in the community still remember his skills. Annie Boutilier's daughter, Kathleen, was eleven when she fell and injured her back while skating at Marriott's Cove. Her older brother, a great believer in chiropractors, took her to William for treatment. Kathleen described him as a kind man who helped relieve the stiffness and pain in her back, "He was better than any medical doctor," Kathleen said later. "I used to visit regularly for treatments, and I grew to like him and Lila. She was kind to me. Knowing I was born at the Home, she treated me like one of her own. When I would arrive, she would say, 'Well, one of my girls has come back,' and give me milk and cookies."

Kathleen said her mother was fond of Lila, but she knew very little about her private affairs. "So much was kept quiet. We know that now, but then it seemed like the secrecy was necessary to protect the girls." Kathleen says her mother would have been horrified to learn about the selling and starvation of babies.

While the Youngs were scraping by with money from loans, the hotel and William's chiropractic business, pregnant girls in trouble still came to their door occasionally, asking for help. The Youngs, unable to resist, sometimes arranged to keep the girls and their babies in their hotel, and later tried to sell the babies. It was an "underground" adoption business that continued sporadically for five years after the Home had officially closed.

By the mid-1950s, profits from the adoption business had

all but evaporated, and the Youngs owed more than $6,000 to Edward Corkum. They also owed money to the tax department and half a dozen local businesses. Edward Corkum was on his deathbed when Lila and William went to his home pleading for money. "Please don't throw me and my children out on the streets," Lila cried. "If you help us now, the Lord will take care of you. He'll be there for you in your hour of need. God bless you, Mr. Corkum." The last words Edward Corkum uttered to Lila were, "God takes care of those who take care of themselves."

After Edward died, his children initiated legal action against the Youngs to recoup the debt. It was a complicated legal process that dragged on for more than a year. On March 4, 1960, the High Sheriff of Lunenburg County put the Youngs' property — five parcels of land bought in 1926, 1941, 1942, 1943 and 1944, including the ocean-front properties — up for sale in the Nova Scotia Supreme Court. From the limited information available today, it seems that no offers were made. Eventually ownership was transferred to the Corkum family, against the debts owed. The bankrupt Youngs abandoned their home and prepared to leave Nova Scotia.

About this time, Lila and William returned to the Maritime Conference of Seventh-day Adventists to be rebaptized. The Adventist faith states, "he who believes and is baptized will be saved." Repentance is a pre-requisite for baptism. They must "confess their sinfulness, and submit themselves to God." Church archives note that they applied, but there is no indication that they were ever rebaptized.

Before the community realized it, the Youngs simply disappeared. They left East Chester penniless, as they had arrived more than thirty years earlier. Lila was still wearing her fur coat — a memento of their prosperous years — but it was worn and sagging. Two of their five children had moved to Sudbury, Ontario; one went to the United States; their daughter Joy and eldest son, William Jr., remained in Nova Scotia.

Lila and William moved to Thurso, Quebec, a small community roughly thirty-five miles east of Ottawa. Lila, who had learned French from a woman who once worked at the Maternity Home, taught school; William worked as a chiropractor. They stayed there for about four years, travelling each Saturday to a Seventh-day Adventist Church on Spencer Street in Ottawa. People who recall their visits to the church say that William had a keen interest in developing the ideal vegetarian diet, which, for him, included fruit, nuts, roots and seeds.

Not long after they moved away, Ray Corkum, son of the late Edward Corkum, entered the former maternity home. Papers and files were strewn everywhere. "It was a complete mess. The furniture had been sold; some of the rooms and the interior of the five cottages on the waterfront were stripped clean," he recalled. Ray, who died in 1989, thought the papers and files found in the building were personal, probably adoption records that no one should see. "I lit a fire and burned everything except a few old pictures. There were piles of papers and reports scattered over floors everywhere. I decided everything should be burned." On that day most of the records from the Youngs' adoption business were lost forever. Ray Corkum would never know the heartache caused by his well-intentioned destruction.

The Corkum family had trouble selling the former maternity home; no one seemed interested in a huge vacant building in rural East Chester. In the summer of 1961, they finally found a buyer: a real estate agent named John H. Crooks. The purchase agreement stated that Crooks would pay $12,499 for the property known as Young's Hotel, house, barn, laundry and chicken house. But before workmen could convert the hotel into an apartment building, it burned to the ground on the morning of Sunday, September 23, 1962.

Ray Corkum, then in his mid-thirties, was sleeping in the house next door, the Youngs' former residence, when he was awakened by the fire at five in the morning. "I looked out the window and saw the entire building ablaze. Flames were licking out every window on the top floor and into the roof." Ray immediately began searching for the four men who were

Young's Hotel and Rest Home, formally the Ideal Maternity Home, went up in flames, Sept. 23th, 1962. Courtesy: The Chronicle Herald.

staying in the building. "I ran around outside the building, but couldn't find anyone. I was panicking."

As a small crowd gathered to watch, Ray was screaming, "Did anyone see Crooks or any of the others?" No one had. "I just kept running and searching, hoping they weren't inside." Moments later, he found Crooks lying on the ground with his furniture around him. "He was sucking air. He had inhaled smoke while trying to get his belongings out of the building." The other men had escaped safely.

Volunteer firefighters from Chester arrived, but the building was an inferno. Unable to save it, they concentrated on keeping the blaze away from the adjacent three-story home. Ray recalled that several windows shattered and the home was scorched, but amazingly it did not ignite. When the fire was finally out, the former maternity home was a pile of charred rubble. Only the brick chimneys were left standing.

As firefighters wet the burning embers, a small solemn group watched, local people who had known the building through its various uses: the Life and Health Sanitarium — Where the Sick Get Well; the Ideal Maternity Home and Sanitarium; Young's Hotel and Rest Home; the Battle Creek of Nova Scotia — Rest Haven Park.

Ray recalled the hours before the fire when he, owner John Crooks and a few friends were drinking in one of the rooms. "Crooks was trying to light an oil stove. He kept lighting matches and throwing them in the stove. After a while we gave up trying and decided to go to a bar for a few more drinks."

At four-thirty in the morning, after Crooks and the others had returned to the hotel, fire broke out. Chester firefighters suspected it was one of the finest acts of arson they had ever seen, Ray said, "but I have no idea why they said that." Crooks and Ray Corkum always maintained that the fire had not been deliberately set. John Crooks eventually sold the property back to the Corkum family. They bulldozed and buried the charred remains and concrete foundation. All that was left on the property was the three-story house, the Youngs' former home.

Now called the East Chester Inn, it is a stately guest home, unique because of its many windows. The nine bedrooms, once inhabited by Violet Eisenhauer and other pregnant girls, are richly furnished with Victorian-style beds and dressers made of walnut and mahogany. The original birch hardwood floors, laid years earlier by William Young, have been restored well beyond their original condition. Outside there is a crumbling arched bridge passing over a brook that used to flow behind the Maternity Home. The duck pond and lighthouse have been covered with earth. The life-sized ornamental deer and the globe holding the brass baby are long gone.

Several years after their hasty departure from Nova Scotia, William died of cancer and Lila returned to Nova Scotia to resume teaching school near Fox Point, where she grew up. In 1969, during the school year, she was rushed to the Halifax Infirmary Hospital, where she died of leukemia. She was seventy. Lila was buried in the Seventh-day Adventist Cemetery in Fox Point. Her headstone reads, "Till We Meet Again."

Chapter 19

Nova Scotia — Burying Its Past

Court records and living witnesses provide an impressive and detailed record of the Ideal Maternity Home and the bizarre business world of Lila and William Young. Yet an unsolved mystery surrounds the Youngs, and it could remain a riddle forever. There is no doubt about the horrific side of their operation, no doubt about the profiteering, the blackmail, the coercion, the greed, the exploitation of helpless children and the impotence of provincial authorities. But many still wonder how Lila and William Young could intentionally let babies die. That babies were neglected, exposed to contagious diseases and malnourished is certain. Such abuse was witnessed by many young women at the Home and detected by government inspectors. And we know from the first-hand account of former handyman Glen Shatford that at least a hundred babies died at the Home before he left there in 1939. But the Youngs were not convicted on the 1936 manslaughter charge, and there is no indication that any additional manslaughter charges were ever contemplated. Certainly no charges were laid.

Fox Point newspaper reporter Malcolm Phillips spent months investigating reports of criminal activity at the Ideal Maternity Home in 1989. He concluded that a small group knew about crimes committed there but chose to remain silent. "People kept quiet," Phillips said, "because they were so grateful for the business during the Depression that they just closed their eyes. It's local lore around here. Everyone knows some facet of it. Everyone said it was murder."

Unfortunately, we may never know the complete truth. In Nova Scotia there is strong reluctance on the part of provincial authorities to re-examine the sordid history of the Home. There is also considerable public resistance. In the fall of 1988, many in Nova Scotia wondered why the Maternity Home stories had resurfaced in the media so many years after the Home shut down. Older people in Lunenburg County, hearing about mysterious baby deaths throughout their lives, urged journalists to leave the past buried. But when former employees began revealing knowledge of starvation practices at the Home and former handyman Glen Shatford admitted he had buried many of the babies who died there, the media hype was unstoppable. The first story aired on the CBC six o'clock news on November 11, 1988. "It has been a secret for more than fifty years," announced the CBC anchor, "mysterious baby deaths on the South Shore. Now an elderly man says he buried the babies in butterboxes. The babies came from a home for unwed mothers. We have this special report."

The television story, showing Shatford searching for the baby burial grounds, attracted national and international attention. In the *Toronto Star*, Julian Beltrame wrote: "Upwards of 100 babies and one of the most bizarre secrets of Nova Scotia's past lie buried a half meter beneath a scrubby bog adjacent to a Seventh-day Adventist cemetery. The bog at Fox Point down the highway from this seaside resort town [Chester] is only one of three mass burial sites that East Chester locals suspect hide as many as 400 infants."

Daily newspapers as far away as Australia gave reasonably accurate accounts. American tabloids such as *The Globe* had a field day with sensational headlines: "Did hundreds of babies perish in gruesome factory of death?" *The Globe* also carried reports of "three mass-burial sites" containing "the tiny skeletons" of as many as 400 infants. It described the story of the Ideal Maternity Home as one of the darkest chapters in Nova Scotia's criminal history.

After the publicity, some Fox Point parishioners approached the pastor of the Seventh-day Adventist Church and admitted they knew of other transgressions committed by the Maternity

Home proprietors and that they would be willing to talk about them if there was an official inquiry. The RCMP in Nova Scotia began investigating some of the more serious charges of starvation and murder. Detectives scoured Maternity Home documents at the public archives, monitored media reports and interviewed former employees of the Home and elderly people in the community.

Soon after, Nova Scotia Attorney General Terry Donahoe declared that he had not ordered the investigation. Donahoe made it clear that he wanted nothing to do with an investigation that might disrupt the lives of women who had illegitimate babies at the Home. However, a lawyer in the Attorney General's office, Wayne Cochrane, told a different story in a June 15, 1989, letter to Michael Reider:

> *A number of police investigations of the operation occurred, the first in the mid-1930s, and the last just this past year, when the Royal Canadian Mounted Police reviewed the matter at the request of the Attorney General. While nothing had been proven in a court of law, suspicions do exist that the Home may have been associated with improper adoption procedures, among other things. However, given the very long passage of time in this case, the failure of earlier investigations to gather sufficient evidence, and the deaths of the principals in the operation I think it unlikely further investigations will now occur, and even less likely that any charges will be laid.*

Following the publicity with special interest was Lila Young's youngest brother, Cecil, who at eighty-three, was still living in the century-old home in Fox Point where he, Lila and the other Coolen children grew up. The house was as sturdy looking then as it was when Lila lived there. With thinning gray hair, flushed face and ice blue eyes, Cecil was a gentle man, still a loyal Seventh-day Adventist.

Sitting in his kitchen rocker, his back as straight as if he were in church, he shook his head in dismay, perplexed over why there was still so much interest in his late sister Lila. Cecil explained that he was not close to Lila while she operated the Maternity Home, but he believed she was a good person. Rising slowly and with a slight stoop, he shuffled into the living room where Bessie Coolen had taught her children so many years earlier. "I didn't know anything about Lila's business dealings, and I never buried any of the babies, not one. I knew babies had been buried in Fox Point, but I didn't realize they might also have been buried on the Maternity Home property."

"Lila thought she was doing work that was necessary in its day," said Cecil, his speech slow and deliberate. "It wasn't like it is today. There was a serious need for that Home. Lila and I didn't always get along the best, she could be stubborn, but I'll tell you this. She was no devil, no murderess."

Another who was following the revelations closely was Tom Rutherford, forty-eight, from Ridgetown, Ontario. One day, not long after the publicity began to die down, Tom drove to Fox Point and asked some of the locals for directions to the cemetery where babies from the Ideal Maternity Home were buried. Rutherford, adopted from the East Chester Home in 1945 at the age of two, had a twin brother who died at the Home. William Douglas Rutherford's death certificate states that he died at three months and one day old and was buried in Fox Point by Lila Coolen Young. No cause of death was given. When Tom Rutherford arrived at the site, he was unable to find the burial ground. All he knows is that his twin brother is buried somewhere in an overgrown section of woodland and that because there are no grave markers, he will never know exactly where.

The province's chief medical examiner, Roland Perry, initially thought the story was a hoax, but when he realized it was not, he too became interested, "It is a fascinating story that should be followed up, not because anyone would be charged with a criminal offence, simply because historically it is fascinating." He did not think it would be worth trying to find the exact location of the burial grounds because the soft tissues of the babies would be long gone and the possibility of finding bone fragments would be slim. Perry thought the wooden butterboxes would have rotted years earlier, but others disagreed. Archaeologists at the Nova Scotia Museum said that depending on soil conditions and other environmental factors, there is a good chance the wooden boxes might still be intact. It took the digging up of a grave where Violet Hatt Eisenhauser's infant daughter was allegedly buried in 1940 to determine exactly what has been preserved.

Chapter 20

From the Grave

Sitting in her rocking chair in the century-old farmhouse where she was born seventy-two years earlier, Violet Eisenhauer could not shed the emotion deep within her as she read the headline in the local newspaper: "Mother's Day reunites Ideal Home pair." It was the story of a mother and daughter finding each other after a fifty-one-year separation. Violet had read about several reunions in the newspaper that year and each time she felt a pang of envy. In this article, a Windsor mother, Madeleine Gaudette, was reunited with the daughter she feared she had lost forever. Gaudette's pregnancy back in Feb. 1942 had been unplanned, the result of a wartime romance with a Scottish sailor. The night she gave birth to the baby, the Ideal Maternity Home was undergoing renovations. She remembers part of the roof had been torn off in a winter storm. After the baby was born she saw her only once when the daughter of a minister from nearby Lunenburg sneaked the baby into Gaudette's room one night while the Youngs were away. "I just sat and rocked her and rocked her and cried, hoping I could keep her. Little did I know fifty-one years later I'd be sitting here with her right beside me."

Seventy-three-year-old Gaudette was just twenty-two years old when she left her baby at the Home, never to return. She had heard there was a baby cemetery nearby, but it was not until decades later, when she read the book *Butterbox Babies,* that she learned not all of those buried were the result of miscarriages or stillbirth. It was then that she felt a strong urge to begin searching. She and her family placed an ad in the Halifax newspaper, a birthday wish for her daughter, Barb

Potter. Amazingly, Barb saw the ad, recognized the birth date and made contact with her mother. Gaudette is just thankful her daughter is one of the lucky ones who made it out of the Home. The two women, both grandmothers, hugged and began to exchange a lifetime of stories as they shared their first Mothers' Day together.

Violet's heart ached just a little more as she read about Madeleine Gaudette's touching reunion with her daughter. So many searches, so many lost years, so many happy endings. For Violet it was not to be. The longing she felt for her own daughter was taking its toll. The memories of how she was separated from Faith Lu Tanya were fading but never forgotten. She would tell the events of that fateful night in July 1940 repeatedly, to anyone who would listen. How she and Sterling wanted children and had no thoughts of giving up their baby when Violet was admitted to the Home. How Violet chose to go to that particular home for the baby's birth because it was close to where they lived and because Violet liked the idea that a female "doctor" ran the Home. But when Lila Young approached Violet that dark night to tell her Faith Lu Tanya had died suddenly, Violet went into shock. Shock quickly grew into suspicion when one of the other girls in the Maternity Home told Violet about a secretive visit by an American couple. The girl said she overheard the couple tell Lila Young they wouldn't settle for a boy baby, they only wanted a girl. Violet remembered sadly that her dark haired angel was the only baby girl in the Home at the time.

Violet was right to be suspicious about the Young's business dealings. Hundreds of questionable transactions had taken place during the eighteen years the Home was open. The Youngs were notorious for giving false information to the pregnant girls and to adopting couples about the babies. There is a wealth of evidence supporting claims that they were selling the babies for big profits and that the babies who were undesirable, because of a disability or the colour of their skin, were left to die.

People who learned of Violet's loss often wondered how the Youngs could get away with something as devious as stealing and selling a baby. Why did Violet's husband or her parents not demand to see the baby after her alleged death? Why did they not insist on an autopsy? And, if they were so suspicious, why did they not contact the police?

Violet Eisenhauer never gave up hope that the baby girl she gave birth to at the Ideal Maternity Home was still alive.

The answer to those questions will surprise many who followed Violet's long and desperate search for her daughter. It could not have been explained during Violet's lifetime without embarrassing her. The truth as revealed by Violet herself in one of her more trusting moments, is that she and Sterling, who died of a brain tumour in 1960, never married. They were in love and they did want to keep their baby, but they never actually signed a marriage certificate. Violet carefully concealed that fact throughout her life. The death certificate issued when Violet's baby allegedly died contains the name Faith Lu Tanya Hatt, Violet's maiden name.

Violet felt her marital status was private and that knowledge of it would only result in more gossip. She was painfully aware of the shame and stigma attached to unwed mothers. She feared the publicity. It was an unfortunate situation that left Violet and her family virtually powerless when dealing with the Youngs.

Over the years Violet visited the tiny grave where they said Faith was buried, but even as she wept quietly and prayed, she always wondered whether it was really her daughter who lay in the ground. Violet, who fancied herself a creative writer and painter, imagined seeing Faith in the tea leaves, a little girl with long black hair skipping rope. She would see her in the blueberry barrens, picking berries and laughing. She would talk to her every July 7th, and whisper, "Happy Birthday, Faith."

In later years, when the details of Violet's search for her daughter were reported in the local newspapers, Violet convinced herself the only important thing was to find Faith. She dreamed of one of those moving reunions she had read about so often. As she aged gracefully, painting pictures of brilliant blue seas and writing poetry about love and life and loss, quietly and alone, she began to realize she and her daughter had lost the most important years of their lives and that her dream would likely never be realized.

Violet's life story touched many people who saw her as helpless and at times desperate. Violet garnered unusual support, possibly because most searches involved babies looking for parents, not parents searching for babies. Violet attracted people who genuinely wanted to help. Some were complete strangers, others, often survivors of the Home, contacted Violet because they hoped they might actually be her long lost daughter. But always, when they compared birth dates and other vital statistics, they discovered they were no relation at all. Still, they would strike up a friendship with Violet and stay in touch through phone calls and letters for years to come. At times it was difficult to know whether Violet held onto hope because was she was so lonely and desperate for companionship or because she truly believed she could still find her daughter.

Violet's state of mind in her later years made her vulnerable, a fact evidenced in 1992, after her story was published. She was contacted by a man claiming to be a film producer who wanted to document her life in a motion picture. He offered Violet $5,000 for the rights to her story. To Violet, who lived on a shoestring budget, it was like winning the lottery. Without getting any advice Violet signed a contract. She wrote to author Bette Cahill in 1992.

Dear Bette,

... I blew it I think. That William Lee, kept after me, sent a man here, tormented me to sign, and promised me $5,000. I never

heard from him since. I have a contract here signed by him. Just like the one I signed and I think it's a fake. I don't know why this man bothered me. I sure got fooled by him. I don't think there will be a movie or anything else. Oh well, I'll never miss what I never did have.
All the best, always
Your friend Violet.

In 1997, Mike Slayter did not let Violet down. He is the head of Parent Finders Nova Scotia, an organization that tries to match adoptees with their biological parents. Slayter developed a strong, personal interest in Violet's case and led a very public campaign to have the grave where Faith was allegedly buried exhumed, giving Violet renewed hope.

His efforts received support from many survivors of the Maternity Home in Canada and the United States who urged the provincial government to pay $2,500 for the exhumation and DNA testing, but to Violet's dismay the government refused. Letters and e-mails poured into the offices of the Justice Minister and the Premier expressing outrage at the government's insensitivity towards Violet.

"This was a very cowardly response. The whole thing has been just ridiculous, said Mike Slayter. They know damn well Violet can't afford to pay $2,500, but they certainly can," Slayter said angrily. "The government has turned its back on her."

Violet felt helpless. "I can't afford it," she told local reporters. "I'm not going to pay for it, they can just leave well enough alone."

Soon after the province refused to help, an archaeologist by the name of Laird Niven was so moved by Violet's story that he offered to dig up the grave himself, free of charge. The offer must have embarrassed the government because soon after it reversed its decision and agreed to pay for the exhumation. Violet could hardly believe it. She was apprehensive, but eager to begin.

On a chilly afternoon in December 1997, seventy-six-year-old Violet Eisenhauer watched timidly from the graveside at Lakeview Cemetery in Chester Basin as Laird Niven and anthropologist Paul Erickson began digging into the hardened earth. Fifty-seven years had passed since the burial, but Niven was thinking that with DNA testing, identifying any remains he found shouldn't be a problem. "It's a real mystery," he told local reporters gathering on the hill beneath a birch tree. "I find it suspicious she was never allowed to see the baby … and they have a reputation for telling parents their babies were dead and then sending them out for adoption. I really have no idea what to expect."

"I don't want her to be in there," Violet whispered to herself as she shivered in the cold. "I just want her to be still living." A group of people, including a few survivors from the Maternity Home, watched closely as Niven wrestled with old tree roots and stubborn stones, for close to five hours, then gently trowelled away the layers of soil. First, they found a rusty nail. Then, about a metre underground, they spotted what they were looking for, a badly decaying box. It was a wooden butterbox that had rotted over the years in the moist, acidic soil.

As friends and supporters clustered around Violet she didn't shed a tear, she just watched as they gently lifted the small butterbox from the earth. The crowd hushed and strained to see as Niven began to pry it open. Inside they found three tiny bone fragments they speculated could be part of a baby's skull. There was some material that looked like paper and shreds of satin used as a lining for the tiny coffin. Sadly, they found little else. When the light began to fade and the late afternoon grew colder, Mike Slayter drove Violet home and stayed with her awhile to comfort her. He says for the first time in years Violet wondered if she had been wrong and whether she just a foolish old woman who couldn't accept the truth. Her self-doubt was short-lived. "The bone fragments they uncovered could be someone else's … another baby," Violet said hopefully. "They found a button, it might be from her clothes. They had all kinds dead babies around there. She [Lila Young] wouldn't have let the box go in empty."

Mike Slayter remembers Violet wearing a brave face the entire day. She even prepared sandwiches and a pound cake which she brought with her in the morning. In the afternoon Violet left briefly, returning a short while later with a food platter; she instructed Slayter and the others to have a rest and eat. "That was Violet's way," says Slayter. "It helps to explain why she touched the hearts of so many."

The fragments of bone they found were sent away for DNA testing to Bode Technology Group, a Virginia based company that had conducted tests for the FBI. But it would be months before the results came back. Violet accepted the delay with calm and grace. "Time doesn't mean much to me anymore," she said.

When the results of the testing were finally announced hope fell to despair. The testing proved inconclusive. There was simply not enough material to extract DNA and make the comparison with Violet's DNA. "The tests couldn't even determine if the bones recovered were human," said Slayter. "There is a presumption by the lab that it was human remains, but that doesn't necessarily mean the same thing."

Mike Slayter comforted Violet as best he could. "She was relieved a little bit because I don't think she really wanted to think that there would be a match," Slayter said. "She absolutely believed that it was not her daughter. Violet was relieved the ordeal was over so she could escape the media spotlight and return to the security and comfort of her home.

Mike Slayter visited Violet frequently during this period with his two young daughters. He helped renovate the old farmhouse by building a bathroom for Violet. Up until that point she had only a sink and toilet in a corner of her bedroom. Slayter spent hours listening to Violet recount her adventures, her travels to meet beaus in Georgia, Alabama and Vancouver. One suitor in British Columbia offered a marriage proposal but Violet turned him down. Slayter believes Violet declined because she didn't want to move from her home in Chester

Basin. She still believed that one day Faith Lu Tanya would show up on her doorstep.

In 1998, Violet circulated a picture of herself at the age of fifty-seven, the age Faith Lu Tanya would be that year. Violet was hoping someone would see a resemblance. At one point a woman from Indiana, who bore a strong resemblance to Violet as a younger woman, contacted Parent Finders and sent them pictures of herself. The similarities were striking, but blood tests later proved they were not related.

Following that came more bad news. Violet was diagnosed with bowel cancer. Time was running out. She talked little of Faith Lu Tanya in her final days and weeks, Mike Slayter remembers. One day she asked him, "Do you think I will ever get to see Faith Lu Tanya?" but the resignation in her voice was evident.

On Monday, Jan. 8, 2002, Violet Eisenhauer lost her battle with cancer. She passed away at Fishermen's Memorial Hospital in Lunenburg at the age of eighty. Violet went to her grave without ever knowing if the daughter she bore sixty-two years earlier was dead or alive.

Linda Tumblin-Koekman, a relative of Violet's, told a reporter at the time that she thought Violet's willingness to talk publicly about her ordeal had "a large impact" on uncovering the goings on at the Ideal Maternity Home, and that Violet was far too humble a woman to ever accept such credit. "She was a wonderful lady, life offered her a lot of hard times but she made the best of those. She stayed close to a lot of people from the Home over the years ... she was very happy about that and most of them called her Mother."

"It's sort of the end of an era for all of us because she died without ever knowing the truth," said Mike Slayter. "To many of us, she was a pillar of perseverance. She will be sorely missed."

Chapter 21

Family Portraits

Only a stone's throw from the bushes where the butterbox babies lie behind the Seventh-day Adventist cemetery in Fox Point is Lila Coolen Young's grave, cared for over the years by her daughter Joy, who struggles with her past and the allegations against her parents. When reports of the baby burial grounds became public in 1988, Joy was living in West Dover, a small fishing village outside of Halifax. Her unpretentious house sat atop a hill overlooking a bay scattered with fishing boats and wharfs. Alongside the house were a backhoe and other pieces of heavy machinery belonging to Joy's husband Tom, who was in the excavation business.

Joy was not eager to talk about the past; the gossip and accusations against her parents had driven her close to the breaking point. Throughout her life, she had heard vicious stories about her family's business, that her parents took advantage of girls in trouble and that babies had been starved to death. With her round face and wide, determined eyes, Joy resembles photographs of her father, but her stocky build and dark complexion are those of her mother. Tom, with rough hands and wizened face, looks much older than Joy.

Joy was young when the Maternity Home was in business and would not have had knowledge of its inner workings. However, she does have vivid memories of the girls who stayed there and the treatment they received. Her recollection differs from almost everyone else's. "My parents were the best, the very best. I know it. God knows it — that's what is important. Their accusers? The day will come when they'll have to answer to God."

Tom, a likeable man to whom a smile and conversation came easily, tried to support his distraught wife. "Will [Joy's father] helped put the roof on our house; we built this place with our own hands. I thought they were fine people, and our children… they always admired their grandparents. They used to visit and bring presents for the children. They were good to us." Tom and Joy have four children, the youngest of whom is named Lila, after her grandmother.

"When I started going out with Joy, I knew them well. I wasn't an Adventist, but that didn't matter; they treated me good." When Tom and Joy got married, William and Lila had planned to give them land as a wedding gift. "That was before they lost everything," Tom said. "That was a terrible time."

When Tom and Joy were married, Joy, who had completed grade eleven, kept the books for the excavation business. In winter, there wasn't much work, Tom said, only a few graves to be dug. During the lean months, he repaired his equipment for spring. If Lila and William profited from the illegal sale of babies, none of the profits, it seemed, had found their way into Joy and Tom's modest life.

Suddenly Joy became angry, almost vitriolic. "I'll tell you what upset me, showing my mother's grave on television. That's disturbing her rest. They're just rattling bones." She stormed from the room, returning moments later with a photo album. Flipping through the pages, she pointed to a photo of her mother's grave. As she studied it, her eyes moistened. "I don't have any regrets; I was proud to be their daughter. We were close. I only wish they were here with me now. We used to have a good life, we were happy. Now it's all ruined. I can't even sleep at night. And our children, how many years will they have to live with this?"

If the fallout from the Ideal Maternity Home caused Joy Young distress, there are many, perhaps hundreds of middle-aged and elderly men and women in Canada and the United States for whom the subject is even more bitter. They are the survivors of the Home who were often brought into lives of confusion and deprivation, of anguished and usually hopeless searches for long-missing families.

Betty Caumartin, born at the Home on March 20, 1941, could not be sold because of rickets and other health problems. She has been searching for her mother for more than forty years. During summer vacations, she and her family travelled from their home in Mascouche, Quebec, to East Chester to see the former Maternity Home property. They visited Lawrencetown, where Betty was raised, but no one she has approached has been able to shed light on her search. "Maybe it is because I feel so happy and strong with my husband and children that I can face whatever I find," Betty says. "I always dreamed of finding my mother. Isn't it strange how we always want to find our mothers, but not our fathers? I wonder why that is?"

In July 1983, Betty wrote to the Nova Scotia Department of Social Services asking for help:

> *I was born in Chester at the Youngs' home for Unwed Mothers on March 20, 1941. My birth name was Sheila Rose Marie LeBlanc and I was told my mother was not married and was eighteen years old when she gave me up... While on vacation I went to Chester to search for information, but people there don't want to talk about these things. So now I am asking you to help, if possible. Some people say I might be disappointed if we were to meet, but that's the price I'm ready to pay. If I don't try I'll never know. Maybe she would like to meet her daughter.*

Trevor Townsend, Director of Family and Children's Services and chair of the Adoption Information Committee, responded:

> *We have checked our records, and the only information we have is that your mother was approximately twenty-three years of age in 1941 and was from Digby County... The reason we do not have more information is that the Youngs' home burned down,*

and all the records were destroyed in the fire, as you already know.

Betty published a letter in a Digby newspaper asking the people of the county for help:

All my life I dreamed one day I would meet my natural mother. Now I feel I am ready, if this is possible. This is my last hope. In Montreal they have help for adopted children and they also had many happy results. Every time I read these articles I keep saying to myself, maybe one day it will be my turn. I guess you have to be adopted to know just how one feels. Maybe it's a hopeless dream, but who knows, if I don't ask for help I will never know. There's no need to say how happy I would be if you could fulfill my dream. If for any reason I find her and she wished it to remain confidential, there would be no problem. Whether she is rich or poor, it makes no difference. I'm not good at composing what my heart would like to say, but I'm sure you will understand my feelings."

Betty did not receive a single response to her newspaper appeal.

Betty Caumartin's dream was still very much alive in 1997 when she approached Parent Finders Nova Scotia to ask for their assistance. Mike Slayter's partner Faith, known by many as the "digger from hell," took what little information Betty had, made three phone calls and astonishingly located the birth family Betty had spent thirty years searching for. Tears of joy flowed freely as Betty and her mother met and embraced for the first time in Mike and Faith's home.

But even the fulfillment of dreams can bring heartache. In the years that followed, the relationship between mother and daughter was bittersweet, mainly because Betty's existence had to remain confidential. Her mother, still suffering from the shame and guilt that came with having an illegitimate child, was unable to reveal her long kept secret to family and friends.

Betty respected her mother's wish. Over time, however, Betty's existence became known, and she was finally able to meet three half-brothers, her cousins and an aunt.

Betty's mother passed away three years later. Today Betty recalls the joy, the hurt and the pain associated with finding her mother. In the end, she says, it was all worth it because finally she was able to shine a light on her past and, to Betty, that is what became most important. "For me the circle is now complete," Betty says, "I know who I am, where I come from, my medical history and I have a brand new family. What more can one ask for. I came out of all of this very rich in knowledge."

Kate Davidson always thought her baby died at the Ideal Maternity Home because that was what Lila had told her. Kate was living in a small town in northern Ontario in June 1984, when she received a phone call from a woman who identified herself as Sharon Lehmann, her daughter. Kate, stunned by the discovery, agreed to a meeting. Sharon remembers the drive to her mother's home. "I borrowed a friend's car and drove from Toronto. I was calm for the first two hundred miles, but as I started getting closer, realizing it would be minutes before I saw my mother, my hands became sweaty, and I was so nervous. I remember she opened her door and my first thought was that she looked younger than I had expected. She was remarkably attractive, slender with blonde wavy hair."

After moments of nervous confusion, Sharon and her mother felt like old friends, pouring through photograph albums and exchanging stories of the past. Sharon explained that the people who raised her, a middle-aged couple in Timberlea, N.S., were relatives of Lila' s. They had adopted Sharon from the Home after losing their six-year-old son in a barn fire. Sharon's adoption, delayed because of a tumour on her lip, occurred in April 1945, three days before her first birthday.

Kate listened intently as her daughter described the search that finally brought them together. Sharon had begun asking about her birth mother at a young age. Her adoptive parents, devout Seventh-day Adventists, told her what they could, but they did not know what had become of her. As Sharon reached adulthood, she could not recall a moment when she did not yearn for her mother.

In 1964, while attending nursing school in Toronto, she and her classmates were in Ottawa for a weekend, and Sharon went to a Seventh-day Adventist Church. As she glanced across the pews, past the heads of ten or twelve people, she noticed a familiar, heavyset woman, moving slowly to seat herself. It was Lila Young. Sharon could not explain why, but she had never felt at ease around Lila, so on that day she chose not to approach her for information about her mother. Twenty years would pass before she began actively searching.

In her early forties, Sharon, happily married with three children, was raising sheep on an eighty-acre farm in Rosthern, Saskatchewan. She decided to contact Parent Finders, and the search began. She passed on what little information Lila Young had once told her adoptive parents. She had said her birth mother was Jewish and a secretary for a Baptist minister in New Brunswick; the minister was believed to be Sharon's father. But the search was doomed from the beginning. The entire story had been fabricated.

In 1984, a relative of Sharon's adoptive parents, who had always known the whereabouts of Sharon' s birth mother, finally contacted Sharon and gave her an address. After forty years, she and her mother finally met. "She looked at me and said, 'is it really you?' It was so exciting. I had gone there prepared for rejection, at the most expecting a distant friendship… but to hear her tell close friends that she once had an illegitimate child and that I was her daughter made me feel about twenty feet tall."

On the night they met, Sharon had planned to stay at a hotel, but her mother insisted she stay at her home for as long as she could. That evening Sharon felt a childlike sense of warmth and security as her mother explained how she had lost her so many years earlier. Sharon discovered she had six brothers who were eager to meet her, but was distressed to learn that her mother was a widow living alone. The reunion with her only daughter, whom she had given up for dead forty years earlier, occurred on the eve of Kate Davidson's sixty-fourth birthday.

Wendell White, who as a boy endured an horrific life of abuse and neglect after his adoptive mother died of tuberculosis and his adoptive father handed him over to foster home, found out about his birth at the Ideal Maternity Home when he applied for his birth certificate. There was no record of his birth. Thinking there was a mistake, Wendell called his adoptive father and his new wife, Louise. "Of course you're not Wendell White — your name is Terry Russell DeYoung," Louise said. "Didn't your father ever explain that you were adopted?" When his father confirmed the story, Wendell ran to the bathroom and vomited.

Wendell's desperate search for his birth mother started at the Registry of Births and Deaths in Halifax, where he obtained his birth certificate: Terry Russell DeYoung, born at the East Chester maternity home, April 1944. The certificate was signed by the attending physician, Lila Coolen Young, and his mother's name was included: Margaret DeYoung — no stated address.

In the years that followed, Wendell began calling himself by his legal name, Terry DeYoung. A lawyer told him it would be illegal to use the name Wendell White unless he made it legal by paying a hundred-dollar fee and advertising the name change in the newspaper. Terry, not interested in legally adopting a name that had brought him so much pain, wanted only to find his birth mother.

He located the godparents named on his birth certificate, but they barely knew Margaret DeYoung. He travelled to East Chester and was discouraged to learn the Home and all the birth records had been destroyed by fire. He contacted elderly people who had worked at the Maternity Home, but they could not help. They told Terry there were so many babies that they had no idea who the mothers were. Some of these elderly people did not even want to talk about the Home because "they were tired of so many young people coming to their doors looking for information they didn't have." Dejected, Terry drove to Eastern Passage, a fishing village outside Dartmouth, and knocked on doors. Someone had told him a Margaret DeYoung lived there in the 1940s, and he was trying to contact people who knew her, but it was another dead end.

He decided to place advertisements in the Halifax *Chronicle-Herald*. "Anyone having information on the family history of Terry Russell DeYoung please write...."

There was no response. Terry was then told about a woman from Eastern Passage who apparently had three illegitimate children in the 1940s. Her name was not Margaret DeYoung, but she did have a baby at the Ideal Maternity Home around 1944. Certain he was following a solid lead, he began an intense search for this woman who went by the name Violet. He tracked her down in Edmonton, where she was living with her daughter and son-in-law. Terry wrote, explaining his belief that she might be his mother and enclosed a photograph of himself.

When he received a reply a few days later, his hands shook with excitement as he tore open the letter. But when his photograph fell to the ground he felt sick. Violet, then an elderly woman, wrote:

> *Your letter came two days ago. I have pondered over it many times as to why you did this terrible thing to me. How can you say you're not upsetting anyone? You're getting that mob [a reference to people Terry spoke to in Dartmouth] against me. They have lots of skeletons in their closet only God can open. Do you know Terry, making all those accusations, if I had money I could turn this into a court case. I feel sorry for you, but those bad women [in Dartmouth] had lots of affairs. They had no morals, just sadness, jealousy and contempt in their little minds being from Owl's Head and Jeddore, those hideaway places. Terry*

I'm sorry I'm not your mother. I would have told you over the phone had you asked. I would not slam the door in your face. You just came to conclusions so suddenly with the aid of those people. You are right; I am living in Alberta with my daughter and her husband. The baby I had in East Chester was a girl; she lived for three weeks then died and was buried out there. She was baptized (God love her). I read your letter with an open mind, many wouldn't have. We all make plenty of mistakes; I'm still paying for mine. I met a nice man but turned him down. I hope you find your parents, I really mean that Terry. I hold no grudge against you, many would have. No wonder there are so many murders. If you had gotten the wrong person this may have happened to you. Terry, did you ever think of that? I know you are a nice man. I will enclose your picture. This is the hardest thing I have ever done. I sure hope you will find your family. God bless you… have a nice Christmas. Do you know I am crying as I write this? I wish you all the luck in the world finding your mother… you are young… you will.

Terry was terribly shaken. He had quite innocently dredged up painful memories that this women had hoped to put behind her. He was heartbroken. Every lead he had pursued left him with an even deeper emptiness. As a last resort, he wrote to his adoptive father, the man who had raised him the first seven years of his life.

I have always been a loner so to speak, never really belonging to any one family, always on the outside looking in, very envious of friends who had parents, brothers and sisters, a family. I grew up a very lonely person with insecurities. I'm not sure if you are aware, but I am now using my birth name, Terry DeYoung… I have been searching for my mother Margaret ever since I learned of this business. I have come to the conclusion that Margaret DeYoung was a fictitious name. But I did find out that DeYoung was my father's name. I have also learned that he is deceased and has been for two years. I realize that ten years ago when I asked you to give me the names of my parents you may have been reluctant to do so as he was still alive. Now that he is dead maybe you can see your way clear to level with me. I have no intention of disrupting anyone's life. I merely wish to find out who I am and where my family is. Basically, I have no one... no family.

It has taken me a long time to sit down and write this letter to you. I sincerely hope you will give consideration to my request regarding my parent's identity... Again I ask for your cooperation in assisting me in my search as it is extremely important to me. I look forward to hearing from you.

The letter, with Terry's return address, was sent to the Coast Guard ship docked in Halifax where his adoptive father worked, but he never acknowledged it. "I waited and I waited, but there was no reply. I was so disappointed. I don't hold anything against him though. If he called me today and wanted to talk I would be there. I don't hate him even though there were times he really hurt me."

Today, Terry, sixty-two, is a man any mother would be proud of. Handsome and personable, he shows no signs of suffering from any physical abuse, but on the inside Terry's scars run deep. He continued searching for his mother over the years, knowing that his only hope of finding her lies with his adoptive father. Now and then he drives by his home and sees him mowing the lawn. "I want to stop, I want to say to him, 'Please talk to me. Tell me what I need to know." Terry always drives by.

Michael Neil Reider was sixteen months old when he was sold to a family in South Orange, New Jersey, in the spring of 1945. He moved to Canada in 1967. He had always been preoccupied by the thought that his mother had been forced to give him up, but it wasn't until after the birth of his son and curiosity about his roots intensified, that Michael began searching. Michael had always suspected that his adoption, arranged by the Youngs and a New Jersey attorney, William Kreiger, was illegal. Michael located documents that registered his adoption in the state of New Jersey.

> I, George H. Becker, Surrogate of the County of Essex and State of New Jersey, Do Certify, that by Decree of the Orphans' Court of said County, dated Feb. 18, 1947, Albert A. Reider and Florence L. Reider, were permitted to adopt Louis Lawrence McKenna.

But in Nova Scotia, no record of his adoption could be found. Michael became certain he had been taken from Nova Scotia illegally when he applied for and received a long-form birth certificate for Louis Lawrence McKenna; none could be located for a Michael Neil Reider. On Louis McKenna's birth certificate he found his birth mother's maiden name, and in the fall of 1989, Michael and his mother were reunited. Two months later, Michael wrote: "Received photos of my newly found and natural family yesterday — quite a weird and wonderful feeling."

Michael's mother confirmed that she had put him up for adoption when she was just fifteen years old and that the transaction was in fact illegal. Among other things, she had never signed a legal document giving him up, and the adoption was never approved by Nova Scotia's Director of Child Welfare. Even if she had signed, the document would not have been binding, given her age at the time.

Sandy Tuckerman, who as a child found it impossible to adapt to a Jewish upbringing in a New Jersey home, had always been curious about her Nova Scotia roots, but when her three-year-old daughter became critically ill with kidney disease in the mid-1970s, she grew desperate for family medical history. "I was afraid for her life," Sandy explained later. "She was in a coma, and I kept saying to my husband, 'Maybe there is something about my medical background that I should know.'"

Sandy wrote to immigration officials to obtain her immigration papers and her birth certificate. Her lawyers wrote to social services workers in Nova Scotia explaining that Sandy had a sick child and needed non-identifiable information and medical history. But Nova Scotia government officials — who may or may not have had pertinent information — offered no help.

Sandy approached friends of her parents who had also adopted babies from the Ideal Maternity Home. Some became angry, saying she had no right to seek out her biological parents when her adoptive parents had given her such a good life. A doctor, who seemed better able to appreciate Sandy's dilemma, discovered in his children's adoption papers that the Home Sandy's adoptive parents had called the East Chester Foundling Home was also called the Ideal Maternity Home. She contacted Parent Finders in Canada, and became acquainted with Edward Brownell, who told her that without her birth mother's name, the chances of locating her were slim.

In 1985, Sandy received a letter from U.S. immigration officials. Attached was a birth certificate containing names she did not recognize. Attached to the certificate was a note saying, "I hope this helps… H.M." Then she noticed the birth date on the certificate: it was hers.

The release of the document was surprising because the U.S. Immigration Service usually seals or amends birth certificates issued to adopted children, but for some reason, they had sent out her original long-form birth certificate, and it contained her mother's maiden name. To this day Sandy doesn't know if it was sent by mistake or if someone took pity on her and sent her the information.

"I was crazy … I called my husband at work and he came right home, not knowing what had happened. Kim, my little girl, was jumping up and down. She was so excited… the children were involved in this, too. There were tears… lots of tears."

Sandy telephoned Edward Brownell to tell him she had

the information he needed, and within a short time Brownell located three women who went by the name Sandy had given him. The first, living in Maine, was not her mother; she was too young. "When I telephoned her and explained everything she felt so bad," Sandy said. "She was so sorry and explained she couldn't be my mother." The second woman was also ruled out after a telephone call. The third woman, a widow in her mid-sixties, was living in a senior citizens' manor in the Annapolis Valley with her two sisters, who had never been told about her illegitimate child.

Sandy, too nervous to make the telephone call, asked her husband, Arthur, to make it. Arthur asked the woman if the date June 1, 1945, and the name June Ellen (Sandy's birth name) meant anything to her. At first the woman seemed suspicious and refused to answer, but after a short explanation, she replied, yes it does. Arthur said, "I think my wife is your daughter."

"My kids were crying," Sandy said, "and Arthur was shaking his head. Yes! Yes! It's her. I was really shaken. I just wanted to hear her voice, but was afraid I would scare her if I picked up the extension phone."

During that initial conversation, Sandy's mother, still afraid someone would discover her deeply guarded secret, refused to speak to Sandy. Sandy felt her heart sink — her search had been so intense. The only thing worse would have been to discover that her mother had died. She accepted that a reunion might be too difficult for her mother. Still, she kept hoping.

Sandy kept calling and asking for more information. Eventually, her mother explained that the pregnancy had been the result of an affair. After giving up the baby, she learned that her husband had been killed overseas. "It must have been horrible for her," Sandy said later. "It was as though she felt the pregnancy and loss of her baby was punishment for her affair." She never remarried and she never had another child.

During one of her less cautious moments, Sandy's mother, a devout Pentecostal, confessed that she had often felt curious about her baby, and once, while visiting friends in the United

States, had actually telephoned the home of Sandy's adoptive parents. Sandy would have been seven years old. Her adoptive mother apparently hung up the moment she realized who was calling. This information was so overwhelming that Sandy asked to meet her mother. "She asked me what I wanted from her. I told her I didn't want anything except to see her. I wanted her to know she had three wonderful grandchildren who were waiting to meet her. That seemed to have an impact and a meeting was planned."

The reunion occurred in the summer of 1985. Sandy drove from New Jersey to Nova Scotia. "I always felt the instant I saw her I would feel a bond. Even though she was hesitant to meet me, I would know this was my mother — this was the woman who brought me into the world." Sandy could barely control her excitement as she entered the senior citizens' manor and knocked on her mother's apartment door. "I thought this is it... when she sees me she's going to grab me and hug me."

Sandy was not prepared for what she found when the door opened. Her mother, greying hair, and glasses, proper and upright — the look of a retired schoolteacher — just stood there, almost bristling. "I wanted to hug her, but I didn't. It was the most uncomfortable feeling. I mean this was my mother... and there was nothing — no warmth, no bond, no nothing. And I remember she said to me, 'I'm so glad you look like your father.' I felt sorry for her. At first I couldn't understand her coldness, but then I realized I had more than twenty years to prepare for this, and she only had a few weeks."

Sandy's mother showed her through the small, plainly decorated apartment where Sandy's eyes were drawn towards a shelf upon which sat a faded photograph. Her mother explained the man was her late husband, killed in 1945. On each side of the photo were candles. It looked rather like a shrine.

Sandy's mother explained that after discovering her pregnancy and realizing she could not keep the baby, she tried to arrange an abortion. When that became impossible, she turned to her mother for help. Her mother advised her never to tell her father about the pregnancy, then sent her away to stay with relatives. Nearing her due date, Sandy's mother went to the East Chester maternity home, where she worked until the baby was born. On June 1, 1945, she gave birth to twins. June — later renamed Sandy — weighed 7.8 pounds; the other baby died. She did not nurse the baby; instead she was fed a formula that she had difficulty digesting. Lila eventually fed her goat's milk.

Sandy's mother told Lila that she wanted the baby taken out of the country as far away as possible. "It hurt me to hear this," Sandy recalled. "It was as though she was telling someone else's story, not her own. I had to remind myself that she was just being honest with me."

Sandy grew confident enough to ask her mother how she felt about finally meeting her. The response was not surprising. "She said she was glad I was okay, but that she did not wish to maintain a close relationship. Still too afraid someone would discover her secret, she explained that the only way she would ever see her grandchildren was if they met on the highway or other remote place. That was how frightened she was," Sandy said. "I felt so bad for this woman. There was no doubt she had spent her entire life blocking out that part of her past. I couldn't help but think this was probably the first time she had ever discussed the pregnancy — with anyone."

In the midst of the discussion, Sandy's mother pulled open a dresser drawer and removed a photograph that had been carefully wrapped in brown paper. It was Sandy's father. He was still alive but had no idea he had a daughter. Sandy was afraid to ask about her father. Meeting with her mother had been emotionally exhausting. More than twenty years of searching had led her to a woman who would remain a stranger. "She didn't reject me," Sandy said. "She told me everything I wanted to know, but I guess in the back of my mind I hoped for a relationship. I mean she was my mother, but I didn't feel any closeness or any affection for her."

All Sandy learned about her father was that he had been living alone on a fishing boat in southwest Nova Scotia, and that he had never married. To Sandy it seemed sad that two people who spent their entire adult lives single and alone never had a chance to share the child they had conceived. Sandy's father did not have a telephone on his boat, but when she returned to New Jersey, she wrote to him: "Dear Dad, I am your daughter. I am coming to see you whether you want me to or not. I don't want anything from you, I just want to meet you. You have three wonderful grandchildren"

The letter was sent to Maisie Hudson, her father's sister, at Victoria Beach, Nova Scotia. A sprightly and affectionate woman in her mid-sixties, Maisie began receiving her brother's mail during the war and continued receiving it afterwards when he lived on the fishing boat. She usually read the letters over the telephone when her brother called, but Maisie knew this letter was different. She tucked it in her pocket and drove directly to Digby. Maisie adored her brother, and as she watched him grow older alone, she regretted that he had never married and had a family. "It took a few moments for it to sink in," Maisie said, "but before long he was remembering it all. I'd say he was emotional, but he wouldn't let on that he was affected. That's just the way he is, but you could tell he was deeply moved."

Maisie invited Sandy to Nova Scotia so she could meet her father. As Sandy drove along the highway, she slowed down as she passed mailboxes bearing the name Hudson. There were many. "My heart was pounding. I was so scared," she said. Then, as she rounded a bend in the road, she saw a crowd of people at the end of a driveway. They were holding a banner saying Welcome to Nova Scotia. "It was like a dream," Sandy recalled. "These were all my cousins and nieces holding this banner and hugging me. And I knew Aunt Maisie immediately. I had seen pictures of her." Through the confusion, Sandy saw an elderly man with white hair, a ruddy face and eyes that were kind and gentle. She touched her father's hands and in an instant felt the warmth she had been searching for.

As Maisie had predicted, the reunion changed her brother's life. He moved off his fishing boat, bought a trailer and installed

Sandy Tuckerman, adopted by a Jewish couple in New Jersey, returns to Nova Scotia for a warm reunion with her father and other relatives.

a telephone so he could be in close contact with his new-found family. Over time Sandy tried, unsuccessfully, to become closer to her mother, but it was not to be. She did develop a keener understanding of her mother's mindset. She learned, for example, that many of the women who had no choice but to give up their babies at a young age coped by convincing themselves the birth had never happened. Sandy felt sad for these women, especially those who might never know if their babies were sold to wealthy families in the United States or neglected and buried in simple wooden butterboxes in Nova Scotia.

Sixty years have passed since the Ideal Maternity Home was in business, and many of the people once employed by William and Lila have passed away. In the fall of 1989, former handyman Glen Shatford still remembered the day he found a baby's corpse in the Youngs' shed. From the sunroom of his cottage in Fox Point, Glen had a sweeping view of St. Margaret's Bay and was less than a mile from the field in which at least a hundred babies were buried many years earlier.

One gray, drizzly November day, Glen agreed to show cameraman David Archibald and me where he had buried the babies. It had been many years since he visited the burial ground and he seemed interested in seeing for himself what had become of it. Walking up through the Seventh-day Adventist Cemetery, we passed several large granite headstones, and Glen stopped to read aloud the names of departed friends and acquaintances. He went by Lila Young's grave without comment.

He moved slowly, with eyes darting towards the wooded area behind the cemetery. The property we were approaching was owned by the Seventh-day Adventist Church; in the 1930s and 1940s it had been owned by Lila's family. As we made our way toward the scrubby bush where the infants were buried, an eeriness hung in the air. For almost an hour, with face flushed, sweating, Glen fought his way through the tangled, waist-high alder. "I know they're here somewhere. I know they're here," he mumbled. The graves were never marked, Glen said, but he thought he would recognize something, possibly mounds of earth or the circles of rocks used to mark burial plots. "You know, I am beginning to think this whole area has been bulldozed. I can't prove it, but these used to be blueberry barrens and now there's a swamp over there in the back area. That wasn't here before." As he searched, puffing on a cigarette, his breathing became laboured. At seventy-six, Glen suffered from Parkinson's disease, causing him to walk off balance. His thoughts were lucid but his speech was impaired.

Weary and frustrated, Glen abandoned the search, but driving back home he remembered the burials as if they had happened yesterday. "I buried many of those babies myself. Once, I had to bury two on the same day. I didn't have to put them down too deep. Just deep enough so the boxes were underground. I remember the butterboxes, too," Glen said, raising his hands to describe their shape. "The looked like old boot boxes. I don't really know how many babies were buried there. At least a hundred, maybe more. I heard they also buried babies in the woods behind the Maternity Home. I don't know if that's true — it probably is. They had to bury them somewhere in the years before they brought them to Fox Point." He paused for a moment, deep in thought: "I know there was talk of two or three other burial sites close to the Maternity Home — they say three to four hundred babies are buried there."

Back home in Fox Point, Glen settled into his big armchair near a wood stove. His once-strong hands, now tremulous, held a cigarette between stiff fingers. He puffed, thoughtfully, perplexed over the condition of the burial ground or possibly, for the first time, he wondered why so many babies had died.

The last time I spoke with Glen Shatford was in January 1992, when he was seventy-nine and quite ill. His sense of balance had deteriorated and he could no longer venture outside his house. He was bedridden and most of the time strained to speak. But his message was clear. "When are you going to tell people about what happened to those babies?" he asked. "People around here are mad at me for talking about this. They're blaming me, you know. But that's okay, that's okay. You go ahead... you tell people what happened to the babies... tell them everything." Glen Shatford died a week later.

Chapter 22

The Forgotten Ones

Old and regal, bright and welcoming: St. Stephen's Anglican Church sits at the top of a hill in the lovely seaside town of Chester, Nova Scotia, where, in the warmth of the morning sun, Sandy Tuckerman, her Aunt Maisie Hudson, Michael Reider, his wife Norma and numerous others quietly enter the church, the setting for the first official gathering of survivors of the Ideal Maternity Home.

It's a Friday morning in November 1992, and they have journeyed from all over Canada and the U.S. to meet face to face for the first time and to forge friendships that will last a lifetime. The air is tense with emotion and anticipation when, in a moving speech to the congregation, Michael Reider, a survivor of the Home, attempts to answer the question, "Why are we here?"

> We are here today to remember those who are not here. They are not here because many years ago they died; some were left to die, some were made to die. They were our brothers and sisters; they were our sons and daughters. They were the children of our nation.
>
> We come together in this House because it is a visible token of the presence of God. Its beauty is the beauty of Holiness, the Church as champion of justice, mercy and peace. ...
>
> We mourn for the lives never lived,
> for teachers who never taught,
> for nurses who never healed,

> for lovers who never loved,
> for dreamers who never dreamed.
> We mourn them, each and every one, even though we know the names of only a few. Each name is precious, each name a prayer so solemn, so holy it is known only to God.
>
> Their birth was a secret. Their life was a secret. Their slow starvation was a secret. Their suffering was a secret. Their death was a secret. Even their burial place was a secret.
>
> For forty-five and more years the secret has been whispered. It is now time to end the secrecy and remember the dead as the dead should be remembered, with honour and with respect. I pray that the horror of the story that has come to be known as the Butterbox Babies never overshadows the most important of truths. That the Butterbox Babies were real — as real as my children and your children, as real as the children we see in the arms of moms and dads each day. They lived, they smiled, they cried and they breathed this Nova Scotia air.
>
> But, when they no longer had monetary potential they became a burden. No one wanted these babies. There was no one to protect these babies. There were few who even knew of these babies. And so, in this thick veil of secrecy and apathy, they were victimized. They were the ones that were left behind. And, how many of us can say, "There but for the Grace of God, would I be."

It seemed fitting that in the brightness of the morning sun the story of the Butterbox Babies is brought into the open. Michael Reider captured what was in the hearts and minds of every man and woman in the church that November morning. Norma Reider, who had played a pivotal role in Michael's search for his mother, presented a recording of a song she had written, called, "Where Have You Gone?"

It happened in Nova Scotia
where a girl had a lover so dear.
But he sailed on a ship
and he went to the war,
that he'd never return was his fear.
But a child was growing within her,
and she carried the secret alone,
crying out to the one
who had left her behind,
"lover where are you,
where have you gone?"

So she went to a home in Lunenburg,
where in peace she could hide her shame
and her golden haired girl
could be born to the world,
without the fear and the blame.

And they told her to leave her little one
for someone else to raise,
but for years her heart ached
and she heard her girl cry,
"Momma where are you,
where have you gone?"

They say some of them went to New Jersey,
and that all are hard to find,
and that some were merely forgotten in time,
they're the ones who were left behind.

Well, I have my own child before me,
and he's safe in my arms as can be,
and I'll teach him to ask what's important to know.
"Where are the children, where have they gone?"

The shades are down, and he's dreaming,

but the shadows aren't hard to find,
'cause I have this feeling of sorrow inside,
for the ones who were left behind.

Oh where is the girl with the golden hair,
and the boy with the eyes so blue,
and the ones who can't hear his mother's cry
"Baby where are you now, where have you gone?

A palpable silence hung over the crowded church as people fought back the emotion, but the mood quickly swung from somber to excitement at a reception following the service. The survivors greeted each other as brothers and sisters separated by time and distance as they talked about a common past and an innocence that began the day they were born. Stories and tearful embraces drew strangers together and joined them as family. Laughter accompanied photo flashes and memory book signings. The hugs and tears they shared that morning and throughout the weekend would say it all.

Following the service, Norma, Michael and the others drove bumper to bumper along the winding South Shore highway, to the burial site at the Seventh-day Adventist Cemetery in Fox Point, an area overgrown and almost inaccessible. A few people walked over to Lila Young's gravesite, located only a few steps from the resting places of the Ideal Maternity Home babies. Others, who found the visit too emotional, waited and watched from a distance.

Terry DeYoung wrote about the memorial service in a letter to the Reiders a short while later:

Dear Norma and Mike,
I commend you both on the excellent memorial service. I had thought I had acknowledged that I was/am a survivor of the East Chester home. However I would say the true meaning of survivor to me was realized as I sat in church that day surrounded by people sharing a secret.

I was moved as I read the story and listened to your music. It was beautiful yet so sad. I wept not only for me but also for the little ones who were not as lucky as I to have escaped the butterbox journey.

I read each newsletter story several times and get weepy when someone is sharing their experience of having found their family. I try to envision just what it would be like, how I would react and what I would say when I meet my birth mother. I get so excited just thinking about it happening I cannot explain the feeling. Part of me wants to cry because I am so frustrated yet part of me so mad that I refuse to let closed doors stop me …
Take Care and God Bless
Regards, Terry

The events of that first weekend reunion deeply affected many, even some who were unable attend. In December 1992, this letter to the editor appeared in the *Chronicle-Herald*:

Dear Editor,
I wish to thank Rev. Andy Crowell, Rev. Tuck, and anyone else involved in organizing the memorial service for the dear, tiny souls who were buried in butterboxes during those years at the Ideal Maternity Home.

I am convinced my husband and I rescued a tiny nine-day-old boy in June 1945, when we went to the home for unwed mothers and chose, out of 40 babies, this tiny bundle of hunger and unhappiness. We lost our hearts to many there, but this skinny little baby wouldn't let go, so we took him home in a butterbox. He was so starved, his fingernails were purple. We fed him pablum mixed with his milk formula and, eventually, we got him and his hungry little tummy satisfied.

Today, he is a husky man of six feet. He has always been our son and I know he appreciates what we did for him. My husband has gone to his final resting place, but before he went he mentioned we more than likely saved our son's life in June 1945.

Some of the "Jersey Girls" (left to right): Sharon Knight, Riva Barnett, Sandy Tuckerman, Ilene Steinhauer

> *I am wondering if Michael Reider may have been one of the babies we had to choose from to pick our son. By the way, this little fellow was apparently not saleable, because we didn't pay anyone for him.*
> *D.M. Hirtle*
> *Chebogue, N.S.*

In the years that followed that momentous first reunion the survivors kept in contact. A newsletter called "The Search" was circulated, a web page was created, Christmas parties were held and a support group was formed and later incorporated so money could be raised for a proper monument to the babies who died. Their story became even more widely known when a Canadian made-for-television movie attracted 3.2 million viewers, the highest ratings ever for a two-hour movie on the CBC. The group of survivors grew larger every year.

Five years later, on Labour Day weekend in 1997, Natalie

Author Bette Cahill interviews Natalie Hamilton and her sister Shirley at a reunion of the Home's survivors in August 1997.

Hamilton, her sister Shirley, Ilene Seifer Steinhauer, Riva Barnett and Sandy Tuckerman — the "Jersey girls" as they call themselves — were among the 400 people who travelled from New Jersey, Florida, Colorado, Arizona, Texas, Maine, Massachusetts, New York, Ontario, New Brunswick and Nova Scotia to the United Baptist Church in Chester for what was to be the five-year reunion of the Ideal Maternity Home survivors. With their white ribbons proudly pinned to their blouses and lapels, they were more than a little excited and nervous as they greeted the people who had become so important in their lives. Violet Eisenhauer, still searching each face in the crowd looking for her long lost daughter, beamed as she was greeted with hugs and kisses and then more hugs.

"Camaraderie is not a sufficient word," said fifty-two-year-old Riva Barnett of New Jersey. She told local and national reporters who had come to cover the event, "It's a powerful bond. This new-found family validates feelings I've suppressed for years and I no longer harbour feelings of isolation and disconnection."

It had been twenty years since Riva tracked down her

Ilene Steinhauer (top and bottom left) and Riva Barnett, (top and bottom right) were adopted from the Ideal Maternity Home and taken to New Jersey.

birth mother. "A non-event," she calls it. "If you don't mind my asking, dear, how old are you?" was the question her mother asked during their brief meeting. And she laughed when Riva responded, "Don't you remember? You were there."

For Riva, the survivor's reunion was the end of a journey. En route to Canada she stopped at every antique shop between the border and Halifax. Finally, she found the object of her quest: a wooden butterbox, 22 inches long, 10 inches wide, 10 inches deep, from the Lahave Creamery in Nova Scotia. It's in a corner of my bedroom," she says. "It's the first thing I see in the morning. It just helps me get my head on straight and realize what's important and not sweat the small stuff."

The weekend held special meaning for Nova Scotia's Jim Gates and his sister Sharon Knight, who travelled from her home in Tuscon, Arizona. Theirs was one of three sibling reunions held privately that Labour Day weekend. Fifty-two-year-old Knight was adopted from the Home by a New Jersey couple when she was just five days old. She had no idea about her connection to the infamous Maternity Home until she tapped into the Butterbox Babies website. "I was stunned. I couldn't understand why they were talking about survivors. It's an incredible story." Soon after she began searching for her biological family and before long she located a fifty-five-year-old brother, Jim Gates of Truro, a half-sister and half-brother. Her mother had passed away.

"Now I feel incredible incredibly happy that in one lifetime I've had not one but two loving families. That Saturday night, Jim and Sharon joined the other survivors and friends at the Chester Playhouse for a moving performance of "Aftermath," a play portraying the story of the Ideal Maternity Home.

For Ilene Steinhauer, born at the Ideal Maternity Home June 22, 1945, and later adopted by a Jewish couple from New Jersey, the trip to Nova Scotia was an emotional tug of war, uplifting and disturbing in equal measure. She shared a wonderful time with her Canadian aunts and cousins, but a standoff with her mother was hard to accept. "I'm disappointed," she says. "I wish it could be different."

Ilene Steinhauer said she feels inextricably tied to other survivors of the Maternity Home, many of whom were adopted in the summer of 1945. "We feel related. It's somebody who has lived your whole story." They also realize their adoptive parents may have saved their lives, bringing new meaning to the words they were told as children, "you were chosen."

Steinhauer went hunting for her Canadian birth family prior to 1997 and found receptive relatives, but her mother told a cousin that she wanted to remain in hiding. "I wish my biological mother would have come running with open arms,

'Oh darling, I've been looking my whole life,' instead of a 'Dear John' letter," she said. "But it's a miracle we are all alive."

A letter Ilene had sent to her mother came back in the return mail: "Your adoptive parents are your true family. Please don't contact me again." But Ilene still sends the occasional note. "You have grandchildren," she writes. "Time is passing so fast. Please reconsider."

Ilene and her husband Steve did eventually travel to Nova Scotia for a long weekend to visit her relatives, who could not have been more receptive. She started crying at the airport waiting for the plane and she kept crying during the flight. "All those years wondering about my family and now I was going to meet them face to face."

Her cousins Janice and Don were waiting for them at the airport. Ilene hugged them and just kept staring at them. "I loved Nova Scotia as soon as I got there. It's beauty, history and pace impressed me deeply. I felt so comfortable and serene in my surroundings. It was like home. I needed to see it and smell the air and feel it."

Ilene says she felt such love from her relatives. They prepared dinners for them, took them sightseeing and told her she was the long lost child of their family. Each aunt gave Ilene a gift when she left, Nova Scotia teacups and saucers and a pewter necklace. She was deeply moved by their generosity and love.

When Ilene returned to Nova Scotia for the big reunion that Labour Day weekend in 1997, she helped unveil the 1.8-metre granite monument dedicated to the babies who died at the home. The monument, located next to the Maternity Home property, was covered in flowers almost instantly. Ilene's birth mother apparently watched the segment on television that night.

"Revealing the secret surrounding my birth has set me free," Ilene later told a New Jersey newspaper reporter. "I no longer feel any shame. I have connections to so many others now. I have answers to the questions about my past, new relatives and very importantly, a medical history. I feel so grateful to have survived and blessed to have found new love from my biological family and other survivors."

Before the reunion weekend was over many of the survivors had one last mission. They wanted to walk over the property where the Ideal Maternity Home once stood, many returning for the first time since leaving there as infants so many years earlier. It was a moving scene as one after another stooped to examine the remnants of the foundation left behind when the Home burned to the ground in 1962.

One woman knelt down and ran her hand through the overgrown blades of grass, picking out small fragments of stone and cement. She stared at the pieces in the palm of her hand as though she was staring into her past. To her these were not just crumbled bits of rock; they were symbols of something large and meaningful. They were the only physical remains of the Home, where she and the others were born, where babies died, where young mothers worked hard to pay off bills and where their adoptive parents came to take them to their new homes. These small fragments from the foundation, which she tucked into her pocket to take home, represented more than most of us can imagine.

Dedicated to the babies who died at the Ideal Maternity Home durng the 1930s and 1940s, this granite monument was erected by the survivors' group in August 1997.

Ideal Maternity Home Reunions

Lorne Franklyn Hall, born January 25, 1934 — was reunited with his birth mother, who was living in the United States, in the summer of 1998. Lorne lives with his wife, Nancy, in North Carolina.

Charles Sweeney — born November 24, 1934 — was reunited with a younger sister and other family members during Christmas 1998. He lives in Nova Scotia.

Bill Lewis — born March 24, 1935 — has been reunited with his birth mother and is proud to discover his father was Mi'kmaq. Bill lives in Nova Scotia.

Donna Levy — born August 8, 1935 — was reunited with her birth mother on her fifty-eighth birthday, at which time she received fifty-eight gifts, all individually wrapped from her mother to mark the occasion. Donna lives in Nova Scotia.

Janice Street — born January 6, 1937 — is the adopted sister of Donna Levy and has been reunited with her birth family. Janice is living in Alberta.

Vance Harnish — born January 25, 1937 — has been reunited with a cousin. He lives in Nova Scotia.

Donald Anthony — born September 26, 1938 — was reunited with his birth mother in 1945 and maintained contact until her death in 1986. He met his birth father in the 1970s.

Mary MacGregor — born September 17, 1939 — and later boarded at the Maternity Home, has been reunited with her birth parents.

Gloria Stolze — born April 18, 1940 — has found her birth mother and siblings, and is searching for her birth father.

Everett Feindel — born August 20, 1940 — has been reunited with his birth family. Everett lives in Nova Scotia.

Brenda Dawson — born December 26, 1940 — was able to contact her birth mother several years ago but her mother was reluctant to continue regular contact. Brenda lives in British Columbia.

William E. McGavin. — born January 30, 1941 — was reunited with his birth family in May 2002. Bill lives in Germany.

Joan Lazell — born March 2, 1941 — has been reunited with some family members. Joan lives in New Jersey.

Betty Caumartin — born March 20, 1941 — met her birth mother in 1997. Betty lives in Quebec.

Nelson Spencer — born August 1, 1941 — has been reunited with his family. Nelson lives in New Brunswick.

Barbara Potter — born November 7, 1941 — was reunited with her birth mother in 1993, after her mother placed a "Birthday Wish" in the local paper on her fiftieth birthday. Barbara lives in Nova Scotia.

Irma Vanderzwaag — February 1, 1942 — has been reunited with her aunts. Irma lives in Ontario.

Helen Irwin — born March 6, 1942 — has been reunited with some members of her birth family and continues to look for others. She also has a brother who was adopted from the Ideal Maternity Home who has already been reunited with his family. Helen and her family live in New Jersey.

Jim Parlee — born April 15, 1942 — has been reunited with his birth family. Jim lives in New Brunswick.

Jane Richard — born April 16, 1942 — has been recently reunited with members of her birth family. She lives in New Brunswick.

Danny Bellefontaine — born June 4, 1942 — has been reunited with his maternal birth family. Danny lives in Nova Scotia.

Rose Neil — born July 8, 1942 — was reunited with her mother and many cousins in April 1998. Rose lives in Nova Scotia.

James VanderMeer — born July 9, 1942 — has found his birth mother. James lives in New York.

Phyllis Roberta Gaye Parks — born July 16, 1942 — met her birth mother and brother in 1987. Phyllis lives in Nova Scotia.

Joseph Bellefontaine — born August 11, 1942 — was reunited with his birth mother on June 11, 1994. She passed away in 1998.

Gregory Keith Haines — born November 16, 1942 — has been reunited with his birth mother. Greg lives in New York.

Robert Norse — born February 6, 1943 — has been reunited with his maternal birth family. Robert lives in Nova Scotia.

Gerald Randall — born February 24, 1943 — has been reunited with at least four siblings. Gerry lives in Nova Scotia.

Donald Wood (Shea) — born May 22, 1943 — was reunited with his biological mother in August 1997. After fifty years of thinking he was an only child, he was in fact an eldest brother to fourteen siblings. On his first birthday after he had been reunited his mother, she sent him a card for every year they had been apart! Fifty-five birthday cards, each with details of what had happened in that year. Donald lives in New Jersey.

Kathleen Boutilier Benedict — born June 16, 1943 — was reunited with her birth mother in Palm Bay, Florida in August 1999. She has since been reunited with several aunts, cousins, and other family members. Kathleen lives in Nova Scotia.

Cheryl Gratto — born August 20, 1943 — has been reunited with two sisters and a brother. Cheryl lives in Prince Edward Island.

Laurine Phillips — born September 20, 1943 — was reunited her birth mother in July 1998. Laurine lives in Ontario.

Natalie Helen Hamilton — born September 26, 1943 — has been reunited with her three birth brothers and an older sister, all in Canada. Natalie lives in New Jersey.

Janet Mason — born April 4, 1944 — has been reunited with her family. Janet lives in Nova Scotia.

Marilyn Fanjoy — born April 5, 1944 — was able to locate information about her birth mother in November 1999. Unfortunately, her mother had died two months earlier. Marilyn lives in Ontario.

Judge Leonard Glick — born May 4, 1944 — was successful in his search for his birth mother, Cora Kennedy. She had been told her son died after a difficult birth, but in reality, he had been adopted by a Jewish couple from the Bronx. Judge Glick and his mother were reunited in 1997 and have a wonderful relationship. Judge Glick lives in Miami.

David Vosburgh — born May 18, 1944 — discovered his birth mother in New Brunswick. She is now deceased but he has been reunited with an aunt and cousins in Ontario, two brothers, one in New Brunswick and one in England, and a second cousin in Nova Scotia. David lives in New Jersey.

William Truffa — born June 9, 1944 — has been reunited with his birth family. He lives in New York.

Penelope Anderson — born September 15, 1944 — was reunited with her birth mother in 1985. It was her adoptive father who conducted the successful search. Penelope lives in New York.

Dena Hiltz — born September 22, 1944 — her birth parents were deceased but she was able to meet her siblings and an aunt. Dena lives in Nova Scotia.

Rita Harris — born September 24, 1944 — has been reunited with her birth mother. Rita lives in Cape Cod.

Carrie Matheson — born October 1, 1944 — was reunited with her birth mother, who was living in New Brunswick in 1997. Carrie lives in Ontario.

Lena Scallion — born October 23, 1944 — has been reunited with family members. Lena lives in Nova Scotia.

Jay Heisler — born November 21, 1944 — was reunited with his birth family in August 1997. Jay lives in Vermont.

Mary Langille — born December 10, 1944 — has been reunited with her biological parents.

Sandra Roper — born December 18, 1944 — was initially reunited with her birth mother and sister by telephone on

June 14, 1998. Sandra lives in Nova Scotia.

Michael Reider — born January 21, 1945 — has been reunited with his birth family. Michael lives in Ontario.

Dale Shack — born March 9, 1945 — has been reunited with his birth family and now lives in Florida.

Catherine Wright — born March 21, 1945 — has been reunited with her biological sister and her children. Catherine lives in Ontario.

Daniel Willett — born March 29, 1945 — has been reunited with his birth mother. Daniel lives in Nova Scotia.

Joel Cox — born May 2, 1945 — was reunited with members of his birth family May 19, 1997. Joel lives in Nova Scotia.

Alice Gess — born May 12, 1945 — has been reunited with family members. She lives in New Jersey.

Sandy Tuckerman — born June 1, 1945 — has been reunited with her birth mother and father, her Aunt Maisie Hudson and other relatives. Sandy lives in New Jersey.

Marta Lewis-Law — born June 7, 1945 — was successful in finding her birth family in 1998. Marta lives in Nova Scotia.

Sharon (Marilyn) Knight — born June 10, 1945 — was reunited with two brothers and a sister in August 1997. Sharon lived in Nova Scotia from 1999–2005. She now lives in Green Valley, Arizona.

Riva Barnett — born June 21, 1945 — has met her birth mother and has established a connection with nieces and a nephew from her paternal birth family who reside in Alberta. Their bond is strong and it will continue. Riva lives in New Jersey.

Ilene Seifer Steinhauer — born June 22, 1945 — has been reunited with some members of her birth family. Ilene lives in New Jersey and is still searching for her father, Carl Colstead of Ontario, a former petty officer in the navy. Ilene's birth mother's maiden name was Myrtle Jane Foote and she was from Red Island, Newfoundland. Ilene lives in New Jersey.

Robert Hartlen —born June 22, 1945 — has been reunited with his birth parents. Bob lives in Nova Scotia.

Joanne Crandell — born August 1, 1945 — was reunited with birth siblings in July 2001. Joanne lives in Ontario.

Richard Meisleman — born August 13, 1945 — has been reunited with a birth sister.

David Garfield — born August 25, 1945 — has been reunited with his birth family. David's sister, Stephanie Lou Garfield, also adopted, died from lupus at age ten in March 1956. David has made contact with members of her birth family. David lives in Hawaii.

Diane Watson — born October 8, 1945 — has been reunited with her birth family. Diane lives in Nova Scotia.

Gail Titus — born November 4, 1945 — was reunited with her family in March 1998, after a search initiated by members of her biological family. Gail lives in Pittsburgh.

Susan Kusnet — born November 15, 1945 — was reunited with her birth family, which includes five siblings, in 1998. Susan lives in New Jersey.

Howard Cooper — born June 3, 1946 — was reunited with his mother Hilda Saulnier (Sweeney) around 1985 and kept in close contact her. Hilda passed away in the spring of 2004. Howard spoke at his mother's funeral and told everyone he was proud to be her son. Howard lives in Louisiana.

Rose Murray — born November 28, 1946 — has been reunited with her birth family. Rose lives in New Jersey.